A Rose of the Sharecroppers

A YOUNG GIRL'S FORMIDABLE JOURNEY OF ADVERSITY AND COURAGE

GEORGIA SHINGLES

ISBN 978-1-64458-951-9 (paperback)
ISBN 978-1-64458-952-6 (digital)

Christian Faith Publishing, Inc.
832 Park Avenue
Meadville, PA 16335
www.christianfaithpublishing.com

Front cover design by artist, Michael Anthony Brown.
Back Cover Photo by Kenneth Shingles.

Quotations by Charles R. Swindoll taken from "When God Closes a Door," January 18, 2007, Dallas Theological Seminary, Copyright © 2007 by Charles R. Swindoll, Inc. All rights reserved worldwide. Used by permission.

All scriptures listed, preceding each chapter are taken from the Kings James Version.

The hymn, "A Shelter in the time of Storm" was taken from the SDA (Seventh Day Adventist hymnal), page 528.

Printed in the United States of America

"A gardener tends the rose
Pruning with love and care,
His eyes must never grow weary
A frail one may be there.
The pests will surely set their trap
To conquer rose and thorns
But, oh, the fragile little rose,
Must live, die and be reborn."

—Georgia Shingles

Bryant and Willie Mae Mack

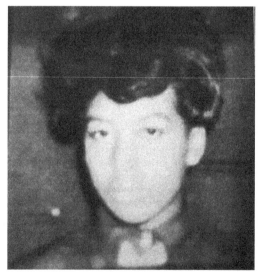

Georgia in her senior year of high school

Acknowledgments

This journey of writing would not have been possible, without the leading and guidance of God's Holy Spirit, and the support of my family and special friends.

To my father, Mr. Bryant Mack Jr., and the memory of my mother, Mrs. Willie Mae Mack. Thank you for your guidance, faith, sacrifice and prayers that shaped me and my siblings, and left a mark of resilience in our children.

Thank you my husband Dave, for allowing me to have the private moments to write, even when some of our time was sacrificed that I may fulfill my vision, thanks also for the relaxing fishing trips.

To my sons Terrance, DJ and Kenny – thanks for your loving support while balancing family time and careers. Great insight Kenny with the back cover photo!

To my daughter Kristie – thanks for your loving dedication and commitment as manager and coach, as you balanced a career, family support and mentored children in the community.

I dedicate this book to you my grandchildren: Kingston, Kyle, Justin, Kenna, Daven, Kalani, twins Callie and Jarrett. Thank you for all your smiles and our special times together that motivated me to keep writing.

To Monica, Tiffany, and Natasha, (daughters in law), thanks much for your prayers and encouragement.

To my twelve siblings, Carol, Willie Earl, Shirley, Price, Benard, Ruby Pearl, Jimmie, Ronnie, Bryant III, Len, and the precious memory of our baby brother and baby sister (Joseph and Jackie). Thank you for encouraging me in your own special way. I pray we always remember the sacrifice and perseverance of our parents, that we may soar to greater heights, and leave a legacy for our children and their children.

Thank you Janette Prescod for sharing your expertise and time; patiently editing my book and teaching me to pay careful attention to detail.

For your devoted, prayerful support—thank you Rhonda Johnson, Julius and Florence Oyier and sons, Ty & Timothy, Theresa Bonah, Zella Venable, Erika Johnson, Rebecca Domina, Lisa Richardson, Margaret McIntyre and Elizabeth Duncan.

Thank you Terry Harris for encouraging me, with the special song that renewed my faith in completing this book.

I also dedicate this book to the memory of my dear, best friend, Mrs. Doris A. Wright who desired to read it before she passed. She always encouraged me to press on… I miss you much.

Thank you Michael Anthony Brown, professional artist for devoting your time, talent and energy, to design the ideal front cover to portray my life story. Your kindness will always be remembered. Thanks again.

Special thanks Linden and Marilyn Laurence for your prayers and encouragement to see it through.

I wish to thank Christian Faith Publishing and the staff that helped produce my book. Special thanks to Leslie Fox, publishing agent for your patience, communication and help during the whole editing process. As of this writing, I can't believe we are almost done!! Thanks again.

Contents

Introduction

A *Rose of the Sharecroppers: A Young Girl's Formidable Journey of Adversity and Courage* begins with my story as a young girl, who was so fascinated with nature, the woods became my second home, and ends with the story of my adulthood. As a young girl, I was fondly called Sal. I played until I heard the familiar voice of my mother. "Where are you, child? Come on home. It's getting dark!"

I was a pure tomboy, and my secluded life, despite the cotton fields, provided a peace I couldn't find at home.

My world was surrounded by the deep woods, the cotton, corn, sugarcane, and vegetable fields. My siblings and I were sheltered by the overprotective care of our parents and strictly reared to obey Christian principles. Cotton was the major crop in the Deep South, therefore it provided a livelihood for poor, uneducated families.

Our sharecropping family plowed and worked the fields under a demanding landlord. Half of the crops were returned to him, and our family survived off the rest. Our parents envisioned an education for us, but field work was priority, and studying nightly by the fireplace was secondary.

From my earliest years, I suffered hearing loss, ill health, and low self-esteem; but I was determined to overcome through my love of books and a desire to please my strict, overprotective father under the rules of the home.

My driven vision to teach prompted me to work hard academically and competitively. However, my sheltered life failed to prepare me for the traumatic adversity that awaited my uncertain future.

The "wounds of disappointment" as referred in my book took me on a formidable journey. I questioned my sanity and struggled to meet every obstacle with the principles taught in the home, the two-room schoolhouse, and the little Baptist church.

My mind was plunged into an arena so shocking and painful I sought refuge in a strange city. Instead of solace, my life became a constant struggle to survive amidst the perils of the environment. This resulted in years of depression and the thought of taking my life. I embraced an adult world so fearful; I compromised principles (that were to protect me) due to a confused and battered mind.

The experiences of the city still served as a triumphant lesson despite the adversity.

With a struggling faith, and strict upbringing, I survived; but returned home, with additional scars. The challenges that awaited me further tested the fibers of my soul. My depressed mind and choices brought me into premature motherhood and the realization that, despite the obstacles, I must survive for my child—though the painful past and haunting memories clung to me like glue.

In the midst of my conflict, as a young woman/young matriarch, I left home again. The driving force behind this departure was my little consoler, my heart, who depended upon me to survive, be courageous, and return for him. He was my bridge between faith in God and the threat of insanity that endangered our future.

These experiences enabled me to walk by faith, to believe the impossible, and to follow God's purpose for my life. Many lives would be touched through my God-given resilience, my family, church, community, wherever I traveled, even the stranger along the way.

In my own words, I compare my life-molding experiences as a "rose." "For a rose to grow, mature, and blossom, it must have tender care requiring the gardener's constant attention to every detail. During its season, the rose will bloom, and die, only to be reborn again."

As a conscious gardener, my Heavenly Father continues to care and nurture me, the rose, until one day I will fully bloom into a beautiful, resilient Christian character giving glory to my Creator.

To those who have lost their way due to life challenges and wrong choices, you are not alone. In many ways, I identify with you. My path and experience typifies many a youth, runaway, and single mother who suffered depression, rejection, loneliness, and a desire to be understood and loved.

However, it sets a precedent that despite the odds, we can grow and embrace with faith an unpredictable future and leave an unforgettable legacy of resilience.

In conclusion, *A Rose of the Sharecroppers: A Young Girl Formidable Journey of Adversity and Courage* spotlights the endurance of my immediate family with God's leading through the prayers and spiritual support of many prayer warriors.

It serves as a testimony that in the midst of our unpredictable failures is the exact moment to faithfully soar and say, "I can do all things through Christ which strengthens me" (Phil. 4:13).

"As a rose passes through stages and blossoms into a masterpiece, nurtured by its Creator, so are the stages of a family, that blossoms through adversity and resilience, reminiscent of our Redeemer who defines our struggles with His love."

—Georgia Shingles

Chapter 1

THE UPBRINGING AND THE SHARECROPPING

I was born on a small farm in Hinds County, Bolton, Mississippi to Mr. Bryant Mack Jr. and Mrs. Willie Mae Mack on March 3, 1952. Our mother birthed thirteen children, of which I am the third.

Our parents were poor devout sharecroppers with a vision to survive the poverty and ensure we receive an education. It was their hope and prayer we would have fewer hardships than they experienced.

When I was very young, we lived in a nice comfortable house with adequate space. However, there were seven children and two adults at the time. But we didn't own the property. It belonged to an overbearing landlord who required us to work long, hard hours in the fields.

Sharecropping was hard, and it profited us little. What we earned from the crops, half was returned for sharing the land. On the other hand, we learned the value of hard work and strong Christian principles.

We rarely complained about the hot sun because of the consequences. As our parents worked, so did we in order to eat and survive. Besides the field work, we did lots of chores, ate hearty, and did our homework by the fireplace. Every night, we read to our parents before bedtime. I loved reading because it revealed a world outside the woods and cotton fields, also the anticipated day we'd stop farming and be like the families in town.

As children, we didn't understand that hard work was preparing us for a challenging future. We had an advantage over the people in town, such as less traffic and limited exposure to fast living. We grew most of our food and enjoyed Mother Nature's supply of berries, plums, muscodines, wild grapes, and other treats in the woods. We bonded with nature and learned to appreciate our circumstances.

Despite hard work, we enjoyed playful games when chores were done, such as hide-and-seek, the lost handkerchief, here-we-go-round-the-mulberry-bush, climbing trees, and many others.

As a middle child, I always felt like the oddball. I was sickly, suffered low self esteem, stuttered and was always embarrassed by hearing loss.

My three sisters were very attractive, but I felt like the ugly duckling. Cora, the oldest, had long, thick black hair and a magnetic personality. Susan was cute and chubby, and everyone rallied around her. My baby sister Peggy, who sucked her thumb, was cute as well. I hid all my school pictures because they revealed a "nobody" lost in the crowd at home and school.

Mama was gifted in many areas. Her skills in natural remedies kept us well, and her specialty soups and devoted care usually restored us.

My sisters and I performed most of the house chores. We cooked, made the beds, and washed our field clothes in the big black pot in the yard. A washboard and wringer washer was used for the other laundry.

Our other chores included feeding the chickens and pigs and helping Mama prepare and store needed food for the winter. We also cared for our younger siblings.

Her special gift was making a variety of original quilts. Her love, patience, devotion, and spirit were in every stitch. Her work was a masterpiece. She never tired of starting a new design. She always said, "I want my family to have good cover (quilts) during the winter." Her hand-sewed quilts were made from remnants of old denim and a variety of fabrics. "They were strong and beautiful and kept us warm during the cold winters in our so-called shotgun houses. Many friends and relatives were blessed with the warmth of her quilting masterpiece. She sang songs as "Amazing Grace," "Touch Me Lord Jesus" and "There's a Bright Side Somewhere" as she sewed. This special gift from her Creator provided a refuge and peace of mind for cloudy days and her many responsibilities. She rarely had time for herself. Each quilt portrayed a different season of her life: her joys, sorrows, disappointments, prayers, and faith in a God she trusted to help her rear her children.

Our parents were gifted with wisdom despite their limited education. To sit and talk with them was refreshing. People visited our home just to hear their counsel. They were our heroes of reading and writing. They could read practically any book presented to them. Daddy wasn't much on writing, but it was one of Mama's gifts. She wrote fast and legible, and her letters were engraved on our soul. Often, we found a letter or note under our pillow containing a dollar or some special word of praise. Sometimes, it was a reprimand and the consequences.

Years later, when we started our own families, Mama continued to write us, and we cherished every letter. Some of us have her memoirs today in those letters. Sadly, some, including family photos, were destroyed in our present home due to a flood in the basement, taking a part of my heart with it. Today, when I find her letters, I sat and listen to her timely counsel. How we miss that great matriarch who amazed many through her wisdom, letters, and humor.

Mama was a great storyteller. Her stories always left us spellbound. She told them with such passion and spirit that left a lasting impression.

One story was about a kind man who helped the poor and homeless. He supplied food, clothing, and whatever was needed to make life bearable. One day, the kind man died. Many people didn't have the missionary spirit, including some church people. His church decided to have a grand funeral to commemorate his charitable spirit. They mourned and grieved because he had touched many lives. A variety of flowers were also donated to his memory.

A friend of the deceased decided to attend the funeral and offer a tribute. When he entered the church, he was greeted coldly, because of his smelly, raggedly clothes and intoxicated manner. However, he paid little attention. As he walked toward the casket, he noticed many flower arrangements. Suddenly, he was approached by two members who asked, "Where do you think you're going?" He told them he came to see his friend and had something for him. So he kept walking. When he reached the casket, the homeless man decided to put something inside. One of the members who were really upset by now said, "You can't put anything in the casket." The poor homeless man said in his grieved, drunken state, "I don't know why not. If my friend here can smell all these flowers y'all got in here, I know he can eat this soup." When Mama finished, we laughed! However, she firmly cautioned us never to look down on anyone and always help others.

Our mother was also a friend and missionary to anyone she met. If she knew of a need in the community, she always found something in our humble home to assist. She instilled in us that we can always help in some way, even if it's a kind, encouraging word.

Daddy lectured us daily on family and spiritual principles to keep us on the right path. It was to our benefit to listen and take note, or suffer the consequences. Most of us strong enough to hold a plow helped in the fields. We had to hold the plow steady to keep the rows straight. If they were crooked, we had to plow them again. It didn't matter how hot or tired we were. After the plowing, we planted the crops. When the cotton, corn, and later sugarcane (which were our major crops) began to grow, we used a long-handle hoe to remove grass and provide additional soil around the plants. Because we dealt with several kinds of grass, chopping around the plants was challenging. The crap grass was the most aggressive. When we chop it one day, the next day it has taken root again. When our crops were caught up, we helped our neighbors and friends and socialized in the fields as we worked.

When we picked cotton, our father required a certain amount each day. Sometimes, he rewarded us. Other times, it was just part of the work because it had to be done. Sometimes the landowner and his sons weighed it to make sure it was accurate. We always held our breath and hoped we had met our quota. If we didn't, we received a whipping. The next day, a larger amount was required. We thought our parents were cruel to make such demands. We didn't understand the more we picked, the more we had for ourselves.

We were ashamed for the landowner's sons to see us in old field clothes and hats, because they always looked fresh and clean. The boys were our ages and size. We felt they looked down on us like we were slaves. Their father drove his tractor to the fields to make sure we stayed on task. He reserved the right to say when to come and go to the fields. If our parents were sick, the crops still had to be worked. Mama didn't like the way he talked down to Daddy. She prayed for the day when we'd have our own place. It didn't matter if it was an old shack. She just wanted our family to be treated decent. Our parents never looked he or any white people in the eyes when they spoke. It was a sign of pride or disrespect.

Our precious secluded home in the woods sheltered us. There was plenty of space to run and play and good wholesome food to eat. We rose early at sunrise and went to the field while it was cool. Usually, we worked until noon. Then we'd stop to eat lunch. We had pinto beans, sweet potatoes, and corn bread with a glass of Kool-Aid. Other times, we enjoyed watermelons and other vegetables right off the vine. We rested awhile and returned to work. We also ate baloney sandwiches and orange crush sodas as a treat from the little country store down the road. We wore wide strawhats to shield our face from the hot, blazing sun and old pants to protect our legs from scratches and mosquito bites. The pants did little for me. I was allergic to the grass and the mosquitoes. I scratched profusely. It left large sores on my legs every year, resulting in impetigo. I stayed embarrassed about my problem. One day, Mama took me to a specialist in Jackson, Mississippi, who prescribed a special cream that healed my condition. However, even to this day, I carry many of the scars…

We disliked working in the cotton fields, because we wanted to be like the other children who didn't have to work as hard. We didn't understand that the hard work and training was setting the stage for important decisions for our young and adult life. I am forever grateful for our parents who instilled in us godly principles in the midst of all their challenges. Thanks, Mama and Daddy!

One day, our parents decided they had enough of the landowner's demands. They packed all our belongings and left the nice house in the deep woods. We moved to an old shotgun house. We continued to sharecrop, but our landlord was kinder. However, he didn't fix up the old house as before. We still had to work hard, but the burden didn't appear as heavy as before. The rest of my life through junior high school was spent picking cotton as the sharecroppers' daughter.

When people visited our home, they referred to Mama as Ms. Willie Mae or Ms. Bill. They addressed our father as Mr. Bryant or Mr. Mack. Mama made folks feel welcome with her delicious meals, popular sweet potato pies and cakes. She timed us on our chores while she cooked. She never missed a beat. She rarely used a recipe because it was in her memory. She was a fast, competent cook. People often asked how she cooked so fast. Her response was, "My crumb snatchers," as she fondly called us, "are always waiting to snatch the crumbs when the food is ready."

Even though Mama used special remedies, she wasn't too proud to see a doctor, if needed. Often, she ran into some of our friends she hadn't seen recently. They shared long talks because we were there for hours. The doctor's office had two entrances.; One for the whites and another for coloreds (as the sign read). There was one doctor in town, a husband-and-wife team. The doctor appeared nice; however, his wife made sure we knew our place. She spoke harshly and reminded Mama the doctor would see us when he could. From our side, we saw the white patients check in and received special greetings and attention. They saw the doctor first even though we had arrived earlier. If we had morning appointments, it would be late in the evening before we arrived home. Sometimes, we waited so long we forgot why we came. When the doctor finally saw us, we were feeling better.

Discipline and respect were major principles in our home. Disrespect was not tolerated in any form. We were taught to address our parents and adults as, "Yes, ma'am," and "Yes, sir." Nothing less! Whenever we misbehaved, we knew what to expect. We were whipped for almost every consequence. Our parents kept switches in the corner as special reminders. Often, we were sent to get the switches. If they were too small or too short, they would send us to get longer and larger ones. We never wanted Daddy to get one, because he brought the largest and longest one on the tree.

We preferred Mama's whipping to Daddy's. She was strict like our father but had a big heart. She made a lot of promises like, "The next time you do that, I am going to whip you good." We didn't realize those promises added up. When the cup was full of promises, Mama grabbed us and switched the living daylight out of us. She whipped us, saying, "Didn't I tell you a hundred times that I was going to get you?"

Daddy, on the other hand, didn't promise much. His promises were short, rare, and sure of fulfilment. He whipped long and hard. He paused between whippings and talked which was pure torture. We knew our parents loved us, but sometimes, we felt Daddy lived just to whip us. He used a switch, a piece of electric cord, or the old-fashioned leather belt. If I had a choice, I would choose neither.

My siblings and I feared our father because he was so strict. He wanted to be such a good parent and us to be good children. We always felt he overdid it. Still we loved him and believed he loved us because he was a good provider. Sometimes, he talked to us about his childhood and how strict his parents were on him and his siblings. His face grew very sad. We often saw a kind side of our father when he played with our younger siblings, bouncing them on his lap and laughing. He also liked to dance occasionally with Mama. That made all of us happy and feel special.

One day, I learned a very painful but valuable lesson when I was about seven years old. Daddy was whipping me across his lap with a belt. I cried and screamed because I was afraid of him. All of a sudden, I did the most foolish thing. I stopped crying and called him, "Fool dog, fool dog." I don't know where I got that from other than my older siblings, who were always daring us younger children to do something. The more I called him names, the harder he whipped. Mama finally said, "That is enough. You have made that child hysterical. Please stop." He finally stopped and reminded me never to do it again.

Mama took me in her arms and soothed my sore bottom and legs. However, I did learn a valuable lesson, never to call Daddy names. When we went to school, we had whelps and bruises on our legs and backs. The teachers noticed but said nothing because whipping was allowed in school. They believed that strict disciplining was the mark of good Christian parenting.

When the crops didn't bring in enough money to support our large family, Daddy went on the road to work construction and carpentry. Sometimes, he was away many days.

Mama and us worked the crops. We had some relief from his whippings and tried to be good because we wanted a good report from Mama. When he came home, we greeted him with a bittersweet welcome, eying one another, hoping we had passed the test. He wanted to know everything. He greeted Mama in the kitchen with a hug and closed the door.

One day, I got myself in big trouble when Daddy came home. He was in the kitchen with Mama. My siblings dared me to listen through the door. I was supposed to report back to them. Because of my hearing problem, I got real close to the door and listened. She gave him a thorough report. Suddenly, I became numb and lingered too long, paralyzed in the position. I couldn't move!

Suddenly, the door opened. I looked right in my father's face. He said, "If you want to hear, then come on in." Daddy gave me a terrible whipping for eavesdropping. The bad thing was, Mama wasn't reporting anything about me. I had brought it all on myself, listening to my older brothers and sisters. I stayed angry with them for many days.

Our oldest sister, Cora, stayed in trouble and got more whippings than any of us. She was determined to do things her way and often paid a big price, more whippings. She was tough, though, and bounced right back. When she was in high school, she kept late hours despite our parents' curfew. They wanted her home at a certain time and not a minute later. She and our parents had lots of battles about that.

When our parents ran errands, we were given chores and told to have them completed before they returned. However, we whispered among ourselves about how unfair they were. We were so foolish. We didn't know how blessed we were. Despite the strict discipline, our parents laid a strong foundation for us. In some ways, we use the same blueprint for our children today, teaching them respect, to excel in their schoolwork, to respect their elders, to read and study God's Word, and to obey Him. They also say, "Yes, ma'am," and "Yes, sir," to adults, and my life stands as a testimony today. I hope and pray that any young person reading this book will please take note of this. Today, I stand on God's promise, "And we know all things work together for good to them that love God, to them who are called, according to His purpose" (Rom. 8:28).

Our oldest brother, Tim, was very mature and talented for his age. He learned to drive by the age of ten. Mama applied for her license but failed. It was years before she passed. While living on the first landowner's place, Daddy reluctantly gave Mama a driving lesson. We convinced him to let us ride along.

He piled all of us in except the baby, who was asleep in the house. They decided not to awaken him since Mama was practicing in the large cow pasture in front of our house. Also, we wouldn't be out very long. It seemed harmless at the time.

Mama drove all over the pasture, and Daddy yelled at her to turn this way and that. We were hanging over the seat, not knowing the danger we were in. Suddenly, Daddy yelled for Mama to miss the pond. She swerved, missed it, and ran into a tree. We got out unharmed and wide-eyed as Daddy checked us and the car.

Mama cried and ran into the house and checked on the baby. He was fine and still asleep. She said, "I'm never gonna learn to drive." When she realized we could have been killed with the baby alone in the house, she cried again. After that ordeal, she stopped being so anxious, still believing the Lord would work it out somehow. Our father decided his nerves had enough, so our brother Tim became her instructor.

Years later, with his patience and the Lord's, Mama came home with her license. We were so proud of her. It was a great accomplishment. She laughed and cried at the same time.

Mama rarely took driving as serious as most people. To her, it was a way to get from one place to another without much fuss. She drove with her elbow hanging out the window and singing her favorite hymns. She also drove in the middle of the road and wondered why people didn't stay on their side. Sometimes, she ran in the ditch, and someone had to pull her out. She would ask, "Now how did I get in there? I was always nervous riding with her when she had these episodes. She talked and sang, and then I would say, "Watch out, Mama." Often I had dreams about us running down a big hill or off a mountain. I would wake up shaking and thankful it was a dream.

Mama drove, admiring the landscape, waving to all her friends as she blew the horn, and reminded us to always be good children.

One Sunday morning as she was driving to church, she shared some prophetic news. She quoted the Bible about the world becoming so wicked, that "one day parents would be against their children and children against their parents." I was about seven years old then. When she said that, a chill came over me, and I said, "Never, Mama, we will never be against you or Daddy." Then I moved closer to her on the seat and held on to her as she drove. Now, at age sixty-six, I have lived to see that dark prophecy come true in our homes, churches, schools, communities, and the world (Luke 12:53). Have mercy!

"I had fainted, unless I had believed to see the goodness of the Lord in the land of the living. Wait on the Lord: be of good courage, and he shall strengthen thine heart: wait, I say, on the Lord."

—Ps. 27:13–14

Chapter 2

THE MIRACLE IN 1960

Our mother endured much and had strength beyond her years. Often she worked in the fields until the babies were due. She stayed in for several weeks and later returned to work. However, there was a time when we thought our mother wouldn't survive.

Mama and Daddy were prayer warriors. When we were in bed, we could hear their long mournful prayers for us that became songs, on their knees. We felt protected as we stayed awake and listened to their commitments through prayer. Mama often told us, "Why worry, children, when you can pray? The Lord will make a way somehow. The Lord will provide." And he always did.

In September 1960, our parents' faith were tested. We were sharecropping cane and cotton on the second landowner's place. The delivery of twin babies was near, and when Mama went into labor one morning, something went wrong. Back in those days, midwives still delivered children in the backcountry. It had been a long year of harvesting sugarcane and cotton. Mama worked beside us in the fields as she carried the babies, not realizing she carried two.

Early that morning, she cried and screamed in terrible pain. Daddy tried to console her but couldn't. He knew it was time for her delivery. But neither was prepared for the agony ahead. He made her comfortable and left to get the midwife. Mama lay in bed, suffering. We were told to check on her and stay quiet. Our kind neighbor and friend came over to stay with Mama but could do very little. I peeped in the room and saw our mother suffering. Suddenly, I was afraid she would die and leave us.

Finally, Daddy returned with the midwife, Ms. Marie. She was dressed in white uniform and white shoes. She had the face and smile of an angel and always spoke so kindly. I can still see her face in my mind today. However, when she was brought to Mama, she couldn't deliver one of the babies. The umbilical cord had wrapped around his neck, and he was dying. It seemed hours before Ms. Marie and Daddy could get her to the hospital.

By the time they reached the hospital, our little baby brother had died. However, the other baby, Little Jerry, survived. Mama was very weak after the delivery. She remained in the hospital weeks before she came home. To care for our surviving baby brother, Daddy took him to his mother. She cared for and nurtured our little brother until Mama came home.

When Daddy brought Mama home, it seemed she had been away forever. She looked very sad. She told us about the loss of our little brother they named James. Then she hugged each one of us.

Daddy brought our grandmother to our home, as she carried Little Jerry in her arms. She had taken good care of him. Mama was seated in her favorite rocking chair. The precious little baby was put in Mama's arms. As she took the baby, she began to sing, "The Lord will make a way somehow." Her body was weak after the delivery and the loss of little James. The doctor advised her not to have more babies. She later said, "I have asked the Lord for twelve babies, and He will provide."

Five years later, Mama birthed four more babies. Three survived, except baby sister Jenna, who lived for two months and died of heart problems. She was a beautiful little baby, with freckles and round cheeks, and a joy for our mama. However, she stopped nursing and stayed fretful, crying much. Mama and Daddy took her to the doctor, and he suggested different remedies to try.

Jenna became ill and began to lose weight. Mama and Daddy took her to the hospital. They were gone all day. When they returned,

Mama's arms were empty. She said little Jenna had gone to sleep. Our little baby sister had died.

We had lost little Jenna too. We thought we were going to lose Mama. She cried and grieved, and so did all of us. Mama's friends tried to console her, saying, "Don't cry, Ms. Bill. You still have other children."

Mama said, "But I wanted this one too."

It was a long time before Mama could go on. She never recovered over the loss of those two babies. Somehow, she trusted God, believing one day she'd see her babies again. That is the prayer of my siblings and mine to this day.

Growing up in a large family was challenging. There was never enough space. Often three or four of us shared the same bed. Every night, we went through a series of "Stop kicking me. Take your feet off me," "Move over. I'm hanging out the bed." We complained until our parents came in and silenced us with the ole familiar switch. Even during my late-teen years, when our grandfather was with us, Mama had bunk beds on one side of the kitchen. She did it in such a way not to embarrass our brothers.

During my childhood and preteen years, I often felt lost in the family shuffle. I ran in the woods, climbed trees, and tried to figure out why I was here. Often I'd roll on the ground, look at the sky, and talk to God, saying, "You really made me. Am I real? Are you really up there, God?" I stayed in the woods until I heard my mother's voice far away. "Come on home, child." I believe God was really listening to me.

"And thou shalt teach them diligently unto thy children, and shalt talk of them when thou sittest in thine house, and when thou walkest by the way, and when thou liest down, and when thou risest up."

—Deut. 6:7

Chapter 3

The Doors of Wisdom

As children of devout Christians, we were strictly trained in the home, school, and church to be respectful to others.

Typically, a week in our home consisted of attending school when we could, going to church every Sunday, picking cotton and vegetables, and performing chores. We missed school regularly to help manage the crops. Our school consisted of a small two-room schoolhouse, adjacent to our small Baptist church. We worked hard to catch up and usually did very well. I liked my teachers and going to school.

Our school was supervised by Ms. Martin and Mr. Williams, who taught multiple grades. Ms. Martin taught kindergarten through third grade. She was strict but kind to us. She required excellence and did whatever was needed to ensure our success. Ms. Martin was a very special teacher. She was tall, walked stately and spoke eloquently.

She had a special patience with all the children, especially me with my hearing problems. She lived by strong principles and imparted them in her teaching and lifestyle. My favorite subjects were reading, spelling, and history.

Mr. Williams taught fourth through eighth grades. He was also strict. We were afraid of him because he was the disciplinarian. Whenever we misbehaved, Ms. Martin got our attention by saying, "I am going to send you to Mr. Williams." He kept a long switch in his classroom as a reminder of the consequences. I can still see that long switch leaning in the corner. Though he was strict, we felt safe with him. He and Ms. Martin were an extension of our parents and earned their trust as good teachers.

We walked many miles to school despite severe inclement weather. Sometimes, we'd hitch a ride on the back of Mr. Williams's truck, and he'd drop us off at a stop we called a "fork." He drove so fast we had to beat on the truck's cab to get him to stop. Many times he dropped us a long distance from our stop, and we'd have to walk the long way back. We didn't like that, especially our sister Cora.

One day, Cora who's known for taking risks, did a very foolish thing. She said, "The next time Mr. Williams passes our fork, I'm going to jump off the truck, 'cause I'm not walking way back up that road."

Well, sure enough, one evening, Mr. Williams was going unusually fast and forgot to stop. So you guessed it, Cora jumped off the truck and hung on to the tailgate. We banged on the cab for him to stop, but he didn't hear us. Cora still hung on to the tailgate, yelling. Finally, he heard us and stopped. By this time, she had let go and was lying on the side of the road. She was moaning and groaning from scraped hands and knees. Mr. Williams got out and yelled at her for being foolish. After checking her bruises, he took us home. Our parents cleaned and bandaged her up and said, "You don't need a whipping. You've already had one."

Recess time was special at our schoolhouse. We played and enjoyed our time together, especially the outdoors. Our school was located in a wooded area, so we ran the hills, played hide-and-seek, and climbed trees.

One day, something happened on the playground that impacted my sheltered childhood. I was wearing a pretty dress; plus Mama had pressed my hair. I was feeling very special. I didn't realize I had a secret admirer—Brad James, one of my classmates. As I was watching my friends play, suddenly, someone came up and kissed me on the cheek. I was so embarrassed. When I turned to look, it was Brad James, and he was running away.

Realizing what had happened, I started to cry. To make matters worse, the children stopped playing and started teasing me. They sang this silly song, "Georgy Porgy, puddin' 'n' pie, kiss the girls and made them cry. When all the girls came out to play, Georgy Porgy ran away." The more they sang, the more I cried. Then I felt someone's arms around me. It was Ms. Martin, my teacher. She comforted me and said, "Everything will be all right. I'll take care of Brad James." After that, I never felt the same about him. I didn't realize years later he'd reenter my life as a kind young gentleman and help rebuild my self-esteem. He would later disappear from my life, and I would never see him again, just hear of him.

From time to time, we would overhear our parents saying our little school house may be closing. Suddenly, we became afraid. We weren't comfortable around the town children and thought they'd look down on us. Soon we put it out of our minds and either went back to our chores or playing. In our minds, that couldn't happen to us. We were so attached to Ms. Martin and Mr. Williams.

We attended the little Baptist church every Sunday with our parents. Before our father could afford a car, we walked long miles on the dusty road. When we arrived, our shoes were dusty, and our pressed hairdos were sweaty. We were ashamed of our appearance in front of our friends. However, our parents reminded us "to be thankful and not complain." At the time that was little comfort, because we wanted to look like our friends.

To prepare for church, we studied our Sunday school lesson the night before. We got up early the next morning to polish our shoes, do our chores, and eat a hearty breakfast.

Our parents were very neat dressers, especially our father, who was a military veteran. They made hand-me-downs look like new. When they could afford it, Mama took us shopping in Jackson to put clothes in the layaway for special occasions. She made sure our needs were met before she bought anything for herself.

She always prepared a special breakfast on Sunday mornings, consisting of large, homemade biscuits, rice and brown gravy with peach or apple preserves. For dinner, we had fried chicken, cabbage, sweet potatoes, collard greens, crowder peas and okra, and a large skillet of cornbread. The vegetables were grown from our garden. For dessert, we had coconut, pineapple, and jelly cakes. Daddy's favorite was chocolate cake. We made a fire in the old iron stove two times a day to cook our meals. Mama cooked breakfast and dinner at the same time. When the preacher or other guests were invited to dinner, we played outside until the grownups had finished eating and talking. Later, we came inside and ate our meal.

I looked forward to church so I could participate in my Sunday school class. Our teacher noticed my interest and asked me to assist. I was pleased because it reminded me of my father, who taught the men's class, with such distinction. In many ways, I knew I was a lot like him. However, I didn't like to admit it, especially when we got whippings. We weren't allowed to talk or run in and out of church during service. We also had certain times to go to the outhouse. The outhouse was a small makeshift structure used as a restroom for home, church, and school. During my childhood and even through high school, our family still had outhouses. We were ashamed, especially when our visiting friends ask to use the restroom. It was many years before our parents enjoyed inside plumbing.

Our nightly baths were taken in a round bottom or rectangular tin tub. We heated our water in the priceless, old iron teakettle in the fireplace. We had to watch it very closely so it wouldn't boil over and kill the fire. We would be punished and have to rebuild the fire and start over again. If the water was too hot, we cooled it with cold water. Often, several of us took a bath in the same water. The last three or four persons would heat more water and take their baths.

When our well went dry, we depended on the rain to replenish water in the large water barrel. During my last year of high school, our parents hauled water from town in a large barrel in Daddy's truck or the trunk of Mama's car. By the time they arrived home, half of it had spilled.

We carried water from the nearby pond for our baths, scrubbing the floors, washing dishes, and doing laundry. We still had to boil the water in the old teakettle to prevent bacteria.

When Mama washed, she used a small blue crayon called "bluing" to preserve the whiteness of our clothes. It made the rinse water blue and our white and color clothes sparkle. Our clothes were hung on a clothesline, including the fence surrounding our house, next to the cow's pasture, because we had so many clothes. It was never too cold for Mama to hang out clothes. We washed every other day. I believe she prayed daily for God to hold back the rain so the clothes could dry. She handled our clothes with loving care as if we were wearing them.

Our little church left a legacy in my memory. We had an awesome senior choir, that sang from deep experiences. When they sang, I pictured them walking right into heaven. They sang from the joys, sadness, seasons of mourning, racial prejudice, their struggles, and most of all their belief in a God that would never leave or forsake them.

Our mother board was composed of the senior women who wore white uniforms to indicate their status. They sat to the right of the sanctuary across from the deacons' corner. All were men, women, husbands and wives, mothers and fathers from different backgrounds with a common purpose. They loved, praised, and served God for seeing them through another week. Many had barely made ends meet to feed their family. They had shared their resources to make sure other families had food and clothing.

Our deacon board began the worship service with powerful, inspiring, devotions, and prayer. The mother board hummed and led out with songs such as *"When I rose this morning, I said thank You, Lord," "The Lord is my shepherd, and I shall not want," "If it wasn't for Jesus, I wouldn't have a friend."*

The congregation joined in praising and thanking God through prayer. I can see their faces today. When I go back home and visit the little cemetery, where our mother lies, I see the graves and tombstones of many who have gone asleep in Christ. Oh, may we never forget their legacy but make them proud, for they suffered and endured much to make things better for us and our children and our children's children.

"What time I am afraid, I will trust in thee."

—*Ps. 56:3*

Chapter 4

The Change and the Retention

On Sundays and special occasions, we visited Big Mama, our maternal grandmother in Edwards, Mississippi. She told us many stories how our mother and her siblings were reared. She always praised God for his watch care over us. When we made the long drive home, it was always late at night.

Sometimes it had rained. The dampness and gloomy sky reminded me of the visits and sad faces we left behind. I wanted our visits to Big Mama to remain alive in my mind. She didn't have much but always gave us a special gift. She reminded us to be thankful and respectful and say, "Yes, ma'am." As she grew older, we could see the moments with her slipping away.

We also visited our uncle who suffered with health problems. Our visits with his family were special since we lived so far away. Aunt Clara, our mother's sister who lived with Big Mama, was born with mental and physically disabilities. She had a heart of gold and a childlike spirit. Mama always reminded us to be kind to her because she was one of Jesus's special little angels.

We called our father's mom "Mother" or "Muh" and his father "Jid." We enjoyed our visits with them and played many games with our cousins who resided there. Some of our aunts and uncles visited from the city with their acquaintances and family.

Due to ill health, Mother spent much time in bed. My siblings, cousins, and I took turns as we piled in her bed, combing her hair, being near her, even though there was little space. Our adult cousins always had something good cooking in the kitchen, such as greens, cornbread, and pinto beans. Later, we ran the hills and visited the older people in the community. They looked forward to our visits as we learned much about visiting the sick and helping others.

When we visited our maternal grandfather in Jackson, Mississippi, it was a special time. We left the country behind and marveled at the excitements of the city. As children, we never understood why he and our grandmother lived in separate places.

When he visited us, he brought candy and treats and told us stories that seemed real.

One of my favorite was Solemn and Grundy. "Solomon Grundy born on Monday, christened on Tuesday, ill on Wednesday, sick on Thursday, very sick on Friday, died on Saturday, buried on Sunday, and that was the end of Solomon Grundy." Granddaddy had a gentleman's demeanor that captured our attention and left a lasting impression.

Many years later, when he began to experience health challenges, he came to live with us in the country. Somehow, with most of us still at home, Mama had a gift for making space for everyone. This taught us the true meaning of service—even though we had little desire to do it.

We listened to granddaddy's stories many years and learned to appreciate his special wisdom and wit.

Often he walked around the yard wearing his special stocking cap. We'd notice him sitting under his special tree, pondering his past life in the city. He and our mother had a very special relationship. She was always patient with him and taught us to be the same. Sometimes, we complained because we had to wait on him. I would give anything to have that privilege today.

It is a valuable lesson to the generation of today. Treasure your parents and grandparents while you have them. One day, your heart will be full of regrets like mine because you didn't value that time. May God forgive us all. The Bible reminds us, "Honor thy father and thy mother."

Granddaddy looked forward to the special flapjacks we prepared for him each morning. I enjoyed seeing the happy look on his face as he enjoyed his special breakfast.

Whenever we asked him a question, he always pondered a long time before answering. After living with us for a while, his health improved, and he returned to the city. We missed him. However, years later, he returned and remained with us until his final days.

It finally happened. Our little schoolhouse that sheltered us was closing. We had to attend a new school in town. We were very frightened on the first day as we stood in the big gymnasium with other students. We waited for our names to be called, as they assigned us to a classroom.

That day, we stepped into a world we had never known. Most of the teachers were from the city. Some came from our little hometown. Others traveled from the country. The new school had an annex schoolhouse for the lower grades, similar to our old schoolhouse. The teachers were nice, but I felt uncomfortable with the city children. I always sensed they looked down on us because we didn't have nice clothes and pretty hairdos.

As we were adjusting to our new school, something unusual happened one wintry day in the annex. We were having class when suddenly we heard a loud explosion. We didn't know what it was.

One of the teachers ran to the door and said the heater had blown up. Suddenly, we panicked and ran. I don't think we had disaster procedures in place at the time. As the students ran and cried, so did I, wondering where my brothers and sisters were. Then we heard glass breaking. Our tall classmate had dived through the classroom window to escape the crowded room.

The teachers tried desperately to calm everyone, but it was no use. After we were outside, we heard another sound. This time, it was like no other. We all stopped! As we turned toward the sound, we saw another classmate screaming and bleeding from his face. Through the panicked rush, he was pushed against a large nail sticking out of the wall. The nail had triangular ripped out a large piece of flesh near his ear. I felt so sorry for him.

After we were outside, others got help for our hurt friend. By that time, our tall classmate came around the front of the annex. He barely had a scratch on him. We all asked him what happened. He said, "I just jumped out of the window because I didn't know what else to do." We stood in awe and just looked at him. We didn't know what to say, because the annex was very high off the ground.

When we arrived home, we related the whole sad incident to our parents. They were grateful to the Lord for sparing our lives. It took me a long time to get our friend's injured face out of my mind. Every time I saw him, I thought of that dreadful day. However, with surgery and care, he returned to school. As he got older, the scar was a reminder how God spared his life.

Our new school brought new challenges for our parents. The attendance policy was different from our old school. Normally, we were permitted to help with the crops and make up our school work. There were few allowances at this school.

If we had too many absences, it meant retention. However, we still had to help with the crops despite the attendance policy. It was our livelihood.

To deal with my adjustment problems, I drowned my anxieties in books. My favorite hangout was the library. I read a new book every week. Our librarian was very kind and encouraged me to be a good reader.

Our parents always wanted us to be excellent readers so we could learn about the world outside our home.

I loved to read the Bible and books from the school library. One of my favorite was *Little House on the Prairie* by Laura Ingalls Wilder. I also loved poems. My favorites were *The House by the Side of the Road* by Sam Walter Foss (1858–1911), *The Road Not Taken* by Robert Frost (1874–1963), *Stopping by Woods on a Snowy Evening* by Robert Frost, and *Mother to Son* by Langston Hughes.

When I was in the fifth grade, I missed too many days from school due to illness and helping with the crops.

My parents were told that I would be retained. I was ahead of my class in age, since I was skipped from kindergarten to first grade at the schoolhouse. Still, I didn't want to repeat what I had learned already; plus the few friends I had made were promoted to the next grade. I was left behind and alone to build new friends. My self-esteem was low, and I bathed myself in pity parties. I stayed angry with the teacher who retained me and the new classmates who didn't understand my feelings.

When I learned about my retention, I became depressed and bitter. I'm not sure if my parents realized how hurt I was. If they did, they didn't bother me about my attitude. I think they felt bad about the whole situation but had so much responsibility with the crops and a large family.

The following year, I decided to make everyone pay. Even though I was pretty studious, I would do just enough work to get by. I didn't socialize with anyone and dared them to bother me. My bitterness grew, reflecting my poor, but decent grades.

No one really bothered me about it. Often, I heard the teachers talking in the hall about my retention. Some didn't understand why I stayed to myself and wouldn't socialize with the other students. That really disturbed them. I learned through rumors that the teacher who retained me realized that maybe she should have promoted me instead. My behavior was apparent to many, and they knew I could do the work.

That same year, a new history teacher came to our school. Somehow, I was assigned to her classroom. Of course, history was one of my favorite subjects.

Every week, I sat in class and refused to participate. One day, she asked the students about my behavior. Some of the girls tried to explain. "Why didn't she ask me," I thought? That made me even angrier. I just sat and listened.

Another day, she was teaching one of my favorite subjects in history. A great discussion was going on, and I wanted to participate. But I didn't. She asked the students a series of questions. The more they responded, I knew they didn't know the answer.

When I got tired of hearing the wrong answers, I blurted out the correct one. Everyone in the class became silent and gazed at me in shock.

The teacher was proud that I had joined in the discussion. Suddenly, one of the girls blurted out, "She knows the answer because she was in this grade last year." That hurt my feelings, but I didn't care. I decided that day to work to my highest potential, and eventually, I excelled in my classes.

I represented the school in spelling bees and poetic oratoricals and usually came in first and second place. My parents and teachers were very proud that I represented the school and our family in a positive way, despite my disappointments.

Math, however, was a challenge. I had convinced myself that I couldn't do it. Maybe I wanted to be left alone to read and study my other favorite subjects. I often felt embarrassed when I was sent to the blackboard and couldn't work the problems.

I felt like the whole world was staring at me. I was also experiencing greater hearing loss. On many occasions, I just couldn't hear and understand the directions.

However, my big brother Tim was a math whiz. He tried to help me, but I had a big fear of math. On the other hand, I did the same for him in English. He had a terrible penmanship. The teachers had difficulty reading it, but I could. When they asked me to decipher his writing, I felt proud to help.

In those days, two cartons of chocolate milk cost a nickel. One day, Mama gave me a nickel to buy white milk. It was nutritious but didn't taste as good. I disobeyed and bought chocolate milk instead. As I was drinking the milk, Mama showed up at school unannounced and caught me. I was shocked to see her! The chocolate milk suddenly lost its taste because I knew what was in store when I arrived home.

"Take fast hold of instruction; let her not go: keep her; for she is thy life."

—*Prov. 4:13*

Chapter 5

THE MATURING IDENTITY

As I matured, I realized I wasn't an ugly duckling after all. When boys noticed me, I felt special. However, Mama and Daddy were strict about us talking to boys and courting.

I still suffered from low self-esteem and hearing loss. When I was attracted to a boy, I took it very seriously. I missed the closeness of my father because he was so strict.

Sometimes, the boys showed an interest in me but were more attracted to the town girls. They made personal demands to see if I really liked them. When I stood for principles, they lost interest. I remember several who felt that way. On one occasion, a boy was putting pressure on me about an intimate relationship. However, I kept saying no. I just wasn't comfortable about it and wanted to obey and please my parents.

As he continued to apply pressure, I felt obligated to say in a letter what I couldn't say in person, that maybe I wanted to, but were afraid, when actually I really didn't want to.

Somehow, I was careless, and Daddy found it. He gave me a long lecture, and I respectfully said I understood.

However, that wasn't enough. He took out a long, hard, piece of rubber with knots and nodded for me to go to my room. He whipped me so hard. I was left very confused about trying to do the right thing. I tried to tell him I was lying in the letter and really wanted to do the right thing, but he didn't believe me.

That drove a bigger gap between our relationship. It also left me with a confused opinion of sexual matters and a greater need to be hugged, loved, and accepted.

Attending my first prom during the last year of junior high school was a bittersweet experience.

My brother Tim and I double-dated. Our parents wouldn't have it any other way. I was dressed in a pretty pink dress and cute heels. I looked attractive, and my shapely legs really accentuated my entire look. My date was nice and well-mannered, but his intentions were not. When I held to my convictions after the prom, he shifted his attentions to another girl. I was hurt, because I really liked him. The rejection deepened when they flaunted their relationship in my face at school.

However depressed and disappointed I was, I didn't know that one day these principles they sneered at would mold my life for Christ's service for the next fifty years. They would be "*my safe harbor*" where I could run to Christ and be safe. Thank You Jesus!

Junior high school years came and went with many experiences. However, I missed my teachers who saw something in this little withdrawn country girl.

We especially loved our only white teacher because she brought goodies from her store to sell. She always respected us. I don't believe she spoke an unkind word to any student or raised her voice. We never felt like we were any different from her. During recess, we went to her room or out on the playground to buy cookies.

Our music teacher was a pure professional. On some occasions, I sang with the choir if I hadn't missed rehearsals due to absenteeism.

Still those songs echo in my mind, such as "Lo How a Rose Ere Blooming," "With a Song in My Heart," A Poem Lovely as a Tree," "America the Beautiful," "My Country Tis of Thee." My favorite songs were "Exodus," "One World Built on a Firm Foundation," and our class song "O Fare Thee Well, Our Dear Reuben Junior High."

I played basketball for a short time, even though I wasn't very good… I was shy and couldn't understand why everyone was yelling at me on the court. I just couldn't hear them. However, I made a two-point shot one time, and everyone was so excited. Later, I withdrew from the team because my interest was in schoolwork, and I really wasn't basketball material.

My first day of high school was bittersweet. I was excited and nervous. I wore a two-pieced blue and gold walking suit with stockings and low pumps. Mama said I looked very pretty. My self-esteem was pretty high that day. Everything was going well until I went to chemistry class.

Our chemistry teacher decided to do an experiment with some hydrochloric acid. I was sitting on the front row, and he was standing beside my desk. When he poured the solution, some of it spilled on the floor. It also spilled on my legs, but I wasn't aware of it.

Suddenly, he jumped back, and we sighed in shock. Later, when I went to the restroom, I noticed little blood spots on my legs. When I wiped it, the stockings came off in my hands. I suddenly realized that my stockings were literally disappearing off my legs. Evidently, the acid had spilled on my legs also.

When I told my friends about it, they said, "Why don't you tell Mr. Rutherford what he did?"

But I was afraid, because he had a scolding nature.

Later that week, the girls blurted the whole story to him. He asked in his stern voice, "Why didn't you say something, child?" I shrugged my shoulders. Then he did the oddest thing. Surprisingly, he took out his wallet and gave me several dollars to replace my hosiery. I accepted it and thanked him and told my parents of the incident when I got home.

During my sophomore year, my sister Cora and I were invited to a Junior College homecoming. A special bus was reserved to take us there. Mama had bought us new outfits for the trip.

As we prepared to board the bus, an old acquaintance came out of nowhere. When our eyes met, the years flashed back. We smiled! We hadn't seen each other in years. It was Brad James from our little schoolhouse, the boy who had kissed me and ran away.

However, he was a young man now. He was handsome and walked very distinguished. I was still experiencing low self-esteem and hearing loss, so I felt a little shy around him.

He was very complimentary and a kind gentleman as he held my arm when we boarded the bus and sat together. He communicated with me like I was the most interesting and most beautiful girl at the college. We laughed and talked about our episode on the playground from the little schoolhouse long ago.

We paused and reminisced, almost tearful about the little school that was gone and almost forgotten in our minds, and our devoted teachers Ms. Martin and Mr. Williams. He escorted me around the campus and introduced me to his older siblings and friends. He never left my side. When it rained, he shielded me with an umbrella and kept his protective arm around my waist.

As we sat through the programs, I felt so special. Here was someone back in my life to help me feel better about myself and valued my thoughts.

When the bus brought us back, it was late into the night. Everyone was asleep. I had laid my head on his shoulder and was also asleep. When he awakened me, I didn't want us to part or the day to end. He asked if he could visit me at home. I said I had to ask my parents. They said yes immediately. He was also from a very large family that believed in strong Christian principles.

When Brad visited me two weeks later, something had changed. We just couldn't connect. He visited again, and we drifted apart.

Finally, we said our goodbyes. I would never see him again, only in my memory. However, I always had that special day when I felt like the most beautiful girl in the world. I thank the Lord for that day. It resonated in my memory from time to time, especially when I felt alone.

One particular morning, our bus arrived at school very late. We learned that Dr. Martin Luther King, Jr. had been assassinated. The whole day was dark and lonely for everyone. Our whole country was in an uproar. All day, students moved in and out of class, shocked at the news. Everyone was sad and couldn't focus on anything but Dr. King's death.

Even though we didn't know him personally, we felt like a friend had died and our hope with him. Our parents really took it hard. They always felt hopeful during his freedom marches and motivational speeches. That tragic and violent act demonstrated what a hateful world we lived in. However, Dr. King left an awesome legacy that we must press on and become the best we could be.

During my senior year, 1969–1970, we rode a shuttle bus, number 90, from the junior high school to the high school. Our bus driver operated our bus with pride and spirit, and his devotion to the students made him a legend and his bus an icon.

It was also during my senior year that I met a very unusual young man. He was tall as the sky, six feet seven, loud, intelligent, with a magnetic personality, a great basketball player, and with a heart of gold. His name was Hunter Reese.

Everyone loved him. I didn't know it, but later I would too. He won my heart and left an impression that lasted 30 years.

Hunter, Tim and I were in Mr. Melton's homeroom. He and Mrs. Dawson were my favorite teachers. He taught English, and she taught history. They taught with a commitment and passion that made us want to succeed. All of us loved them dearly. Everyone said Mrs. Dawson and I resembled in dress, hairdo, and mannerism.

My assigned seat in homeroom was on the front row two desks from Hunter. He always said something humorous that kept the class in laughter. Our teacher repeatedly sent him to the office, but it mattered little because our principal always sent him back. All our classmates looked up to him, but I couldn't stand him. I was concerned about being studious and ladylike and diligently prepared for college. His personality and mine were extremely opposite. He could embarrass you with the slightest comment.

One day, our assignment was to recite portions of "McBeth" before the class. When I began to recite, Hunter made gestures and comments like, "Tim, man, your sister sure is fine." The whole class burst into laughter, and I gasped for breath. Mr. Melton smiled and scolded Hunter and encouraged me to continue.

Who could recite after that? Mr. Melton scolded Hunter again, and he stopped. Somehow, I stumbled through the recitation and received an A. I'm not sure if he gave me the A for the recitation or the courage to struggle through the whole ordeal.

The taunting and teasing continued. Soon it became evident to our classmates, Mr. Melton, my brother Tim, and most of the school, but little to me, that Hunter wanted me to be his girl. I denied the thought and said, "No way. I wouldn't be seen with that loud unpolished guy."

Our homeroom was known as the most popular class in school. Everyone in the class was either studious or athletic, or both. Mr. Melton was like a father to us. He was strict but very kind and nurtured us as his own children.

As the teasing continued, one day, Hunter and my eyes locked, and I felt something for this crazy guy. I couldn't believe it!

One day, he came to school dressed up, wearing his navy blue blazer just for me. He even carried my books but always made me late for library class. Often, I was scolded for tardiness and walking with a loud undisciplined student.

He was still loud at times but toned down as our feelings continued to grow. One day, while we were changing class, I asked Mr. Melton if he thought Hunter was serious about his feelings for me. He said, "I have known him a long time but never seen him react like this over a girl. Yes, you are special in his life." I didn't know what to think. I turned and walked out the classroom, not wanting him to see me blush, because I felt the same about him.

One day, Hunter asked if he could visit me at home. I said I'd ask my parents' permission. Surprisingly, they said yes. My siblings had already told Mama and Daddy about this guy, tall as the sky that had announced at school I was his girl. They just grinned. By this time, our parents had softened about dating; still we were to conduct ourselves as ladies.

One Friday evening, I heard a car outside. I looked out the window and saw this tall figure walking toward our house. The car had dropped him off and left. He knocked on the door, but I didn't want to open it, because I was wearing an old T-shirt and slacks.

However, my parents said it was okay. He brought me a flower and looked so handsome in his blazer. My heart was beating fast as we looked at each other. I had never felt such love before. He kept looking at me and smiled. I introduced him to my parents, and he visited about thirty minutes before his brother picked him up. Mom and Dad left the door ajar of course.

Before he left, we kissed and sealed our relationship that I was his girl and he was my guy. Then he tried to touch me inappropriately. Before I realized it, I slapped his face so hard it sounded over the room. Then he said, "What? What did I do?" I told him that I don't play that. Then he smiled and apologized. After he left, I counted the hours when we would see each other again. I felt proud that I could demand his respect regardless of my feelings.

Well, the rest is history. However, I must share this part of my life. If it helps some young person make better choices and utilize the brokenness from those choices for a focused life in Christ, then my vision for this book is accomplished. It taught me how God can lift you from despair despite what you're going through and restore you to your created purpose, which is to glorify Him.

Another revelation! It was Christmas, 1969. Our homeroom was having a Christmas party. Everyone shared gifts. I hadn't expected anything from Hunter. Then I noticed our classmates exchanging gifts.

Suddenly, Hunter ran in the classroom and laid a big fancy box tied in pretty ribbon in front of me on the refreshment table and ran out the room. All the girls sighed and prompted me to open the box. I was so nervous, and my hands were shaking. I was also embarrassed about the way he did it.

I finally opened it and discovered a set of scented linen hangers and a gold silk housecoat. They were the most beautiful gifts I had ever received. Our classmates sent up a big cheer because this was a side of Hunter they didn't know. It confirmed in everyone's mind that he was really in love.

I looked at Mr. Melton and blushed, and he said, "I told you." I felt so special that I was his girl. Soon, I was known as Hunter's girl all over the school. Students I didn't know came up to me and said, "Hunter really loves you. He talks about you all the time."

When I attended the basketball games, everyone watched my reaction when he had the ball. However, through it all, I was still shy, and I learned by the end of our senior year, he also was shy in a certain way, behind that loud voice. That made our relationship even special.

Our favorite song was "Someday We'll Be Together" by Diana Ross and the Supremes. He also liked "What's Going On?" by Marvin Gaye. Every day, I couldn't wait to see this tall giant of a guy and his big bright smile. He could easily be spotted in the hallway because he was the tallest student in school. I was so much in love with him and him with me. It was kind of scary, too, because I couldn't believe that someone could love a country girl like me.

Still, it felt too good to be true, like a dream, and I would awake and find it wasn't real. Often, I felt that something would happen to end it all!

One day, he sprained his ankle and couldn't play basketball. The whole school felt sorry for him. My parents looked forward to his visits. They even bent the curfew. Mama valued his visits because she liked their talks, and he loved her country meals. As his ankle healed, sometimes he rode the bus home with us. Even our bus driver welcomed him. We walked from the bus stop together, supporting him on his crutches. My brothers also walked beside him, supporting him. After his visit, they drove him home.

When he was better, it wasn't unusual to see him walking from Clinton to Bolton to see me. We tried not to spend much time alone, but it was hard. We were too emotionally involved. We even talked about our future as man and wife after college.

As the end of our senior year drew near, we found ourselves spending more time together. Sometimes, the temptations were too great! He even went to church with us on various occasions.

My sister Susan's boyfriend Daniel and Hunter were good friends and played on the same basketball team. Often, they visited us together. They enjoyed playing ball with our younger brothers, getting their clothes dusty. When they became tired, they sat on the porch talking to our mom. She talked to them about two hours (using up our time). When it was time for them to leave, Susan and I weren't always happy campers. However, Mama was full of wisdom and knew we didn't need to spend a lot of time alone with those guys. They loved Mama and enjoyed her words of wisdom. Mama treasured those days for many years in her mind. She called them "her boys."

*"The spirit of a man will sustain his infirmity;
but a wounded spirit who can bear?"*

—*Prov. 18:14*

Chapter 6

THE WOUNDS OF DISAPPOINTMENT

As graduation approached, Hunter and I faced decisions about college. Because he was studious and a great athlete, he received many basketball scholarship offers.

One day, I was called to the office to meet a basketball scout that had interviewed Hunter. He refused it unless I was offered a scholarship as well. However, he later accepted a scholarship at a college out West. My heart sank. I was happy for him but sad for myself. At the time, I had applied to Tougaloo College outside Jackson, MS. The day he left for summer basketball camp, I thought I would die.

I cried the whole time. We stayed with him until his flight departed. We held on to each other as if it was the last time we'd be together. In a sense, that was true. But we didn't know it.

A big change was ahead of us. Maybe my tears were an indication of the pain ahead. I couldn't stop crying. I didn't want him to go. He was also looking sad, but we both knew he had to. We didn't know the next time we met, our lives would have changed. We would experience many challenges.

However, God still guided my life. But at the time, I couldn't see it, because we were so focused on each other. The world revolved around Hunter and Peach, as he called me.

When his flight departed, so did my heart. I returned home, took to my bed in tears, and listened repeatedly to "I Stand Accused" by Isaac Hayes and our favorite song, "Someday We'll Be Together" by Dianna Ross and the Supremes. We wrote each other twice a week or whenever we thought of each other. He had the most beautiful handwriting to be left handed.

Hunter had been at basketball camp a few weeks when I received a special letter, saying, "I miss you and want to marry you." I was so excited. We didn't have a telephone, so I called from the small funeral home/barbershop in town. Without any hesitation, I said yes to his proposal. Daddy wasn't thrilled about me going such a distance from the family, but surprisingly he didn't object.

Mama was excited because she worried about my depressed mind. We selected a wedding dress and ordered it right away. I was so happy. We were finally going to be together as husband and wife, even though we didn't have a clue what life was about or what lay ahead.

Mama, my sister Susan, and I planned the wedding. Whatever depression I had experienced was gone, or so I thought. Our small community was also happy for us.

A few weeks later, I received another letter from him, that he had talked with his coach and was told to wait—that we were too young and this marriage would interfere with his scholarship. On that advice, he cancelled our wedding.

I was devastated and shocked. To make matters worse, my wedding dress arrived the same day as the letter. I crawled into my parents' bed, holding my wedding dress and cried my heart out, and returned to my forgotten life of depression—this time heartache and disappointment.

When Mama came home, I was curled up in her bed, wearing my bridal veil that I would never wear as his bride—unable to face life or anyone. How long I stayed there, I don't know. I tried to face people, but it was difficult. My brothers teased that I had been jipped for those pretty Spanish American girls. I also believed it. After all, how could I measure up to them, a little green country girl? My mother also began to have doubts about Hunter.

For the next several weeks, I worried and lost weight, and depression became my best friend. Even though it was time to prepare for college, I couldn't go because I couldn't focus.

It's so strange when I reflect. I truly believe God was leading my life. When I was a child, I walked often in the woods, talking to God about my feelings, wondering why He created me and for what purpose? I didn't feel like I belonged in my large family. I really believed God talked to me. The walks provided solace for my lonely heart.

It was during those walks that I gave Jesus my heart. I didn't realize I had allowed Hunter to take Jesus's place in my life. That as much as Jesus loves me, He's still a jealous God and He alone deserved the glory, honor, and praise. Now I can see how Jesus permitted life circumstances to lead me back to Him, even when it meant losing Hunter.

These consequences took me through experiences of adversity and hardship and many miles from home. But through it all, Jesus supplied the courage to bear it. He did not leave or forsake me. Thank You, Lord! He'll do the same for you, reader.

Hunter came home at the end of summer. I was pale, underweight, and still unsettled about the cancelled wedding. He looked sad and uncertain. I spent our time together trying to persuade him to change his mind. But he wouldn't budge. He kept assuring me that we'd be married in three years.

At the end of summer, he left Mississippi to begin his college career and play ball. I was left with a shattered mind, broken dreams, and no vision—all because I had allowed this man to be priority in my life instead of Christ.

To help my depressed state, our parents decided to send me to visit my older sister Cora in Michigan. They felt Hunter had made his decision and couldn't hold me in a relationship—that I owed no loyalty to him.

However, I felt different. I still loved him and believed he loved me. I felt he had been taken from me, and I wanted him back.

Cora welcomed the idea and invited me to come. She was expecting soon. I was reluctant to go but went, anyway. Hunter also thought it was a good idea.

Hunter called weekly since he worked part-time in a bank. However, we ran my sister's phone bill up to $100. That was a lot of money in those days to put on a phone bill. However, he took care of it.

The train ride was long, tiring, and full of uncertainty. What awaited me there? Could I focus and get a new perspective about my life? Mama and Daddy warned me about talking to strangers, to take care of myself and watch my footlocker.

The wind was icy cold when I changed trains in Chicago. It reminded me of the cold, chilled change that had taken my joy, my future, my wedding. As I rode the train, I felt like I was going to another country with so much uncertainty. I was so afraid but anxious to see my sister. I missed Hunter so much and wondered if I would ever see him again.

The train was taking me far from Mississippi. A red cap was kind enough to help with my footlocker. Mama had packed it with everything. My train arrived in Michigan around 2:00 a.m. I was glad to see my sister. She ran toward me and gave me the biggest hug. I hadn't seen her in eight years. Hunter had already called several times. I was glad to hear that because I felt alone in this strange place. When we arrived at her home, I called him. Still, my heart was troubled. Here I was at one end of the country and he at the other. How could our relationship survive such a distance?

The first day, Cora drove me around the city, introducing me to her friends. They appeared very nice. However, I was shocked to see some of them smoking marijuana right there in the park. I had never seen anyone smoke that stuff before. We had been cautioned at home and school never to touch it. A strange feeling in the pit of my stomach told me that I was in an uncertain situation, and so far from home. What did this mean?

After I was settled at Cora's home, her friends offered to show me around the city. I was reluctant because I didn't trust their intentions, especially after their drugs episode in the park.

However, she and Hunter thought it was a good idea. They had no idea what they were asking. It's strange how everyone seemed to know what was best for me instead of just asking. I loved my sister and was glad to be with her. I missed our talks and time together since she moved away. I also knew that she would protect me, if she knew I was in danger. When we were children, she always came to our rescue if anyone was picking on us at school or on the bus. I always wished I had her courage. I longed for this same security in this city, but I didn't know how to tell her. I wanted to appear more grown up that I really was. She and her husband made me feel very welcome in their home. Whenever she ran errands, she invited me to come along.

Cora's friends called me her pretty, sweet little sister from the South. They teased me about my Southern dialect and being so naïve but still respected me to a point.

On several occasions, I went out with them and participated in things that I knew were wrong like trying beer and staying out late, even into the wee hours of the mornings. I am very ashamed of some of the things I did. And I asked God for forgiveness. I could easily blame my frame of mind on depression. But still I had choices. Even though God honored my choices, He still strengthened me through the consequences, especially when I said no to drugs.

My first experience after seeing drugs came unexpected. My new friends took me to dinner. Later, we visited one of their homes, sitting around and talking. Suddenly, they turned the TV down and the stereo up. Everyone went into the kitchen and left me alone in the living room.

I didn't have a clue what was going on. Finally, a man came and sat beside me on the sofa. He had pans, needles, and syringes in his hand. I sat stunned at what I was seeing. All of a sudden, it dawned on me that these were more dangers I had been taught to avoid.

The man asked if I wanted to get high with him. Suddenly, my whole life flashed in front of me. All my parents teachings came to my mind. I knew if I did this, I wouldn't be the same person. Nor would I be able to look at myself in the mirror the next day. Somehow, I took a risk and said, "No." I wasn't sure how he was going to react, because I was the only one who wouldn't participate.

Then he did the most surprising thing. He reached over, took my arm, and said, "I mean you keep saying no because it's too late for me. Look at all those big pretty veins in your arms. You keep them that way. Now look at my arms. They are all full of holes. Why, I can't even find a vein to stick myself."

It was then I knew I was under God's covering and His anointing by saying no to drugs.

Immediately, I went in the kitchen and found people snort-
ing white stuff and their eyes looking funny. They smiled at me and
returned to the drugs. Dazed, I went back into the living room and
waited for a ride home. By that time, the guy in the living room was
out cold from shooting drugs.

I was numbed and silent all the way home. I wondered how
I could handle all this with a depressed mind. "Will it get worse?"
I wanted to ask them why they were abusing their bodies, but I
couldn't. I was either too cowardly or ashamed because I was with
them. I wanted to ask my sister if she knew about this. But I was
terribly confused and afraid. Actually, I was no better than them.
Perhaps they were experiencing similar challenges and thought drugs
were the answer. It was a sad situation for all of us.

Now when I look back, I hope saying no to drugs sent a mes-
sage to my friends, that there is a better choice and that choice is
Jesus. However, I still felt like I was inside a dark cave trying to get
out, in the midst of depression, heartache, and fear.

Though I said no to drugs, I continued to go out with my new-
found friends.

One night, I was riding with a guy and his sister, and they began
arguing. I was sitting in the middle when he took out a gun, and
mumbled something about finding some guy and getting his money.
He apologized for using profanity and pulling out the gun. Then
they passed huge amounts of money between them. They took me
home and continued their late-night pursuits.

I could have been shot or killed on the streets that night and
thrown in a ditch. No one would have cared or found me. I must
say, in their own special way, they looked out for me despite their
dangerous choices.

Later, when I returned to Mississippi, I learned that this guy
had been killed.

Among all my new friends was a special young man, on leave
from Vietnam. He enjoyed teasing me about my Southern accent.
He had noticed me more than I realized. One day, he teasingly asked
me to marry him. I thought he was teasing, but he kept asking. I
told him about Hunter and that my heart was imprisoned with him

and no one could take his place. However, It was good to know that someone else saw something in this little country girl worth marrying. It just wasn't the right guy.

Through tears for him and myself, I said no. After I returned to Mississippi, I learned that he had been killed in Vietnam. I cried because I felt I had let him down. I will always remember him.

I finally came to realize that I had brought much on myself, through wrong choices. Sure, I could easily blame my sister and Hunter, but in all honesty, all I had to do was say "no." I had done it when I was offered the drugs.

I thought of Hunter cancelling our wedding that brought this pain. But in reality, I had done it—when I allowed him to become first in my life. Actually, everything I did and thought revolved around Hunter. When I slept, ate, walked or whatever I did, I imagined him watching over me, walking with me—that what he thought was priority. The attributes I delegated to this man, belonged solely to Jesus and Jesus alone, who gave His life for me.

Even as I write, I pray for many people, young and old; who have surrendered their identity, their vision, their future to another human being. May our attention focus specifically on Jer. 29:11-12 , "For I know the thoughts that I think toward you, saith the Lord, thoughts of peace, and not of evil, to give you an expected end. Then shall ye call upon me, and ye shall go and pray unto me, and I will hearken unto you.

Little did I realize that God's plan wasn't Hunter's or mine but His. He had a purpose for everything that happened to me. Michigan and my relationship with Hunter was a training ground for me later in His service. He was molding me through each adversity. Little did I know that greater challenges lay ahead.

The depression became greater. Sometimes I didn't know who I was. I was leading a double life. I spent most of the night half awake, crying inside, "Help me Lord. I know you are out there. Where is my future, my life? Why am I here?

Help me somebody!

Even though I shared with Cora, a part of me couldn't let her know that I was not the grown up girl, she thought I was. Her listening did help me much.

When Cora had an accident in the car, I walked everywhere alone. I did occasionally get a ride with my friends, but I refused because I didn't want to be around their drinking and drug usage. I walked often in the snow (after I got off work) to sort out my life with Hunter, the influence of the city, and my relationship with God. When I began to realize I had put Hunter before God, I didn't believe He would forgive me. So my relationship with Him remained uncertain.

I worked part-time as a service station clerk and car detailer. The station owner was kind and offered a ride at times.

I continually felt the need to go to church. I missed the presence and protection of God that I had back home. After all, we were raised in church, and I knew my parents wanted me to go.

One day, I asked Cora about a church. She told me about the little Berean church across the street from her home. So I decided to go.

I really didn't feel fit to enter anyone's church after living such an unstable life despite my battered mind.

One Sunday morning, she awakened me and prepared my breakfast, and I went to church. When I went inside, I felt like I was in another world, that I had been snatched from a war zone into a place of peace and safety. It had been a long time since I'd felt that way. Even the people appeared different. I felt protected. The new faces welcomed me with warmth and kindness. I also participated in the Sunday school class.

The members were amazed I knew something about the Bible and was raised in a Christian home. I wanted them to shelter me from the problems outside. I marveled that this little church was right in front of our house, all the time. I had been so distracted with working out my problems that I forgot to look there for the problem-solver. I felt so secure that I didn't want to go back out there. I wasn't sure I could survive another day.

I worried about my depression and the strange friends who dangerously impacted my life. I didn't have a sense of belonging anywhere. My future had been stolen, and I was living a nightmare and would never wake up.

Something inside me cried out, "Help me!"

While I was there, the members asked me to sing. I chose "Amazing Grace and "Precious Lord." As I sang, I felt God's presence reentering my life. I felt a warmth of assurance that He hadn't forgotten me in this place. The members nurtured me, and I felt special. I made friends with several girls my age. Even the pastor and his family invited me home to dinner the last Sunday I attended. It was a bittersweet visit because I kept thinking about when they would take me home. My sense of belonging was gone.

Oh, how I wanted them to say, "You don't have to go back out there. You can stay here with us. We will take care of you, and everything will be fine."

But I knew that was not possible. I had to leave and return to an uncertain world and survive another day. Through all of the nurturing, there was still a longing for peace, to awaken from this nightmare. Deep inside, I just wanted to be Hunter's wife and love him. I had put so much stock in our relationship that I felt I couldn't function without him. A part of me actually believed that being with him would solve all my problems. What a terrible mistake I made! Not trusting God but putting trust in a fragile human being.

It was like I was living someone else's life and mine was on hold—and for what!

I often asked myself why my world was built around this man so deeply.

Then it dawned on me that I had never felt that close daughter/ father closeness. I was raised obeying our father out of fear, with the constant threat of whippings and punishments. I knew my parents loved us, but I missed that closeness as a middle child. The hearing loss and the constant yelling when I couldn't hear brought low self-esteem.

Our parents did the best they could, and without the training, I wouldn't have survived. When Hunter came into my life, I was finally with someone who cared for me despite my disabilities. For the first time in my life, I felt special attention that I hadn't received at home. His attention seemed to cover that fear. It was a new awakening I had never known, being reared back in those woods, but did not, could not last. I had tried to let Hunter do what God desired to do.

In essence, my confused priorities darkened my spiritual focus on Christ because He had a special purpose for my life. I had put my trust in man instead of God, and this was the consequence.

Slowly, God's promise of Isa. 41:10 began to register in my mind. *"Fear thou not; for I am with thee: be not dismayed; for I am thy God: I will strengthen thee; yea, I will help thee; yea, I will uphold thee with the right hand of my righteousness."* The Bible that I had read beside the fireplace suddenly became alive in my heart. I became hopeful.

I appeal to fathers today! It is so important to love, communicate with, and nurture your children, especially your daughters, so they won't seek attention in all the wrong places, with the wrong people. They can take time and grow as God desires them, not building their life around a person who has flaws also. Today at age sixty seven and a half, there are scars I can't erase because of my immature choices, because I didn't put God first. However, I praise Him for giving me a beautiful family, who I dedicate to Him daily. Thank You, Lord!

I walked many days in the deep snow, talking and crying to God, contemplating my life, and wondering when this pain would end. Sometimes I even sang. I wondered if anyone cared that this young girl was dying inside from depression, loneliness, heartache, and fear.

I also became angry with Hunter. I felt his rebounded decision had driven me from my protected home and family and landed me in the arms of more pain and heartache. I didn't know how to break this chain of circumstances that had me bound. There was no one humanly to share this pain I carried, but there was Jesus. He was there. I just couldn't see it at the time.

Before leaving for Mississippi, I met a nice Caucasian guy who invited me to his place for dinner. I didn't want to go, but Cora thought it was okay. We talked, and he said he liked me. When he kissed me, I cried uncontrollably. He looked confused and asked what was wrong. I told him about Hunter and my depressed life and why I was here. He listened intently and patiently. I was in such an emotional state that I walked to the window of his apartment and said to myself, "Why don't you just end your life right here?" The man felt sorry for me, respected my feelings and state of mind, and made no further demands on me. I thank God he didn't allow him to take advantage of my emotional state. Grace had been extended once again. This time, it was definitely time to go home! He gave me a beautiful pink knit sweater for Christmas and sent me home in a cab.

Two days later, I arrived at the train station. He was one of the ticket agents. We smiled at each other, and I dropped my head as we said goodbye. I never forgot his kind face.

As I boarded the train, I looked back at him and all the experiences I had gone through. The tears streamed down my face as I said goodbye to him and my sister. I really didn't want to leave her. Through my depressed moments, she had been a source of strength in a very special way. I thank the Lord for providing His strength on my confused life.

The train ride was long and full of memories. "Should I tell Mama and Daddy about my experiences, or should I leave that chapter of my life closed?" As I traveled, I looked out the window and cried. "Should I go home or just keep riding?"

The sad farewell from my sister was hard—and the memories, the people, the little Berean church, the guy on drugs, the soldier from Vietnam, and his son. It all stayed in my mind.

Now, somehow, I had to push all of this in the back of my mind and prepare for home. I finally realized that I was returning home in worse condition than before. Very little had been accomplished, or so I thought!

My family and Hunter met me at the train station in Jackson. I think Mama was hoping I would have stayed in Michigan. She knew Hunter hadn't changed his mind. I was glad to be with him again, who appeared more mature and handsome. However, he had no idea what I had endured, even though we spoke regularly on the phone. There were things I couldn't even share with him.

We spent much time together. He still hadn't changed his mind about us getting married. I remained depressed and wondered why I had come back, but where could I go? The loneliness was overwhelming! I felt it even when we were together.

After Christmas break, Hunter returned to school, still content with us waiting. I was left behind again with more brokenness than before, and no way, so I thought to fix it. I was so messed up.

When he proposed that summer, my mind had locked into the intimacy of a man and wife. We had always talked about a little Peach and a little Hunter. Somehow, with the wedding cancelled, I still couldn't shake it. Oh, Lord, help me!

I found myself brooding around the house as before. I worried, cried, and lost more weight. Mama tried to help by taking me to work with her.

One night, I began to experience excruciating pain in my back. First, it felt like severe indigestion. When I breathed, it became increasingly worse. I thought perhaps I was out of shape. I exercised by the fireplace to relieve the pain, but it didn't help. The more I exercised, the pain worsened. Mama massaged my back with home remedies, but no relief came. Finally, she said, "I'm taking you to the doctor in Raymond."

The doctor examined me and frowned. He checked his medical book and told Mama I had pleurisy pneumonia. We had never heard of it.

Somehow, while walking in the snow, and suffering from a weak immune system, I had unknowingly become ill. I know stress played a big part also.

When I left Michigan, it was terribly cold and still snowing. The temperature in Mississippi was strangely warm.

Hastily, I changed from snow boots and winter gear to lighter clothing and didn't realize my body couldn't transition as quickly.

Mama was given strict instructions regarding my care at home. She gave me the medicines and special care, and soon I was on my feet.

I lost more weight as I lay in bed with my mind torn between the past and the uncertain future with Hunter. I wanted to share my burdens with my parents but didn't know how or where to start. So they stayed buried in my mind, behind a wall that I dare not penetrate. It was just too painful! The memories haunted me a long time. I did finally heal physically from pneumonia but remained sick emotionally.

"Have mercy upon me, O Lord, for I am in trouble.
Mine eye is consumed with grief, yea, my soul and my belly.
For my life is spent with grief, and my years with sighing:
My strength faileth because of mine iniquity, and
My bones are consumed."

—Ps. 31:9–10

Chapter 7

THE DEFERRED DREAM, THE REBOUND

In the fall of 1971, my sister Susan decided to enroll at Jackson State College, Jackson, Miss. Somehow, she persuaded me to enroll with her. I wasn't doing anything with my life, and I needed an education. I was going to work with Mama to keep busy and earn a few dollars, but deeply depressed. Hunter was pleased. But for me, it meant emerging from a depressed, sheltered world, and dealing with new situations and people my mind couldn't handle.

Hunter had come home for summer break, but still wouldn't agree to get married. After he returned to college, I knew I had to shake this depressed state, and begin my life. In a sense, I had lost a whole year of my life, so I thought.

I was pale and underweight. My courage and self-esteem was very low. I was still very fragile and afraid of another disappointment.

Susan and I didn't have a dime to our name, but we decided to go on faith. We were eligible for some financial aid, but not enough to carry us the whole year. Still, our parents were very proud.

After starting to school, Susan and I learned that we couldn't share the same dorm room. It was a hardship for our parents because they would had to supply items for two rooms. However, we did have separate rooms with roommates across the hall from each other. I guess this helped us make new friends.

We had grown up together like twins. We laughed and cried together in many situations. When our high school sweethearts chose college careers that left us behind, we cried and mourned together. Mama even dressed us alike, and people actually thought we were fraternal twins. I was tall and slim, and she was short, petite, and cute.

We dislike being apart but accepted it. Susan had two roommates, and I had one.

To lighten my darkness, God used part of my Michigan experience as a testimony during freshman orientation.

I was able to share the "just say no to drugs" experience with the freshman students. It provided a temporary consolation and helped my self-esteem. It also enlightened my sister about some things I had experienced.

We listened and shared experiences how young people can get into trouble with drugs, sex, and all kinds of temptations. As I shared my experience, the students and my sister were amazed. Some appeared shocked. Others seemed to say, "No way."

After the meeting, many students said I was very brave. Some said they didn't believe it happened, because sometimes you can be forced to participate. That no one is a wallflower in a situation like that. I said, "Whether you believe it or not, it did happen, and God knows."

The instructor was proud that I shared such an experience. For the first time that year, my self-esteem was lifted. I had begun to be a witness for Jesus and didn't even realize it. Thank You, Lord!

Mama and Daddy were proud to have us in college, even though it was challenging. We were dirt poor and survived on grants and student loans. After we had been in school for three months, Susan and I received letters that our financial aid was gone. We'd have to drop out of school if we couldn't pay our school bills.

We talked and cried like two little old ladies. Then we remembered something Mama always said, "When you find yourself in need, just ask in prayer. We decided to be brave and plead our cause to the financial aid director. And plead we did. We shared our dilemma, how we as sharecroppers' children were there on faith and a vision. Our poor parents had no money to keep us in school. That if we left school, it would crush their dream. We had made history in our family, being the first of many to attend college.

After we finished, the director and his secretary were in tears. He said, "Mrs....we must find a way to keep these girls in school. This is what educating students is about." They revised our financial aid, and we remained in school.

When we came home on break, Mama loaded us with foodstuff and quilts. There was plenty to share with our roommates. We were called "those special country sisters". They teased us much but had respect for had respect for our values.

Hunter and I continued to call and keep in touch. However, our talks grew into arguments. We argued about being together and anything else we talked about. He wanted one thing, and I wanted another. I was barely making decent grades to stay in school, because I thought of him all the time. When I'd see other couples on campus, my heart longed to be with him. I just couldn't shake it. I was so lonely.

Our arguments grew worse until one night we called our relationship off. Very few people knew it other than Hunter and me. I don't know who he told. I was so depressed I didn't tell anyone. I still wanted to be his girl and one day his future wife. A part of me hoped we would come back together. But a part of me was just tired of the whole situation and the arguments.

I had lost much strength trying to survive. To concentrate on college work with the arguments and my uncertain future was too much. My depressed mind longed for peace and some space from all the pain and disappointment. Part of me would let him go, and another part would bury him somewhere in my mind. Just couldn't take much more!

Still I loved him. I just wasn't focused enough to know what else to do.

During this time, an unusual situation had mounted on our dorm floor. We answered the telephone often for one another. This particular guy, Sean Wolford, called every night for one of our dorm friends. She was never available. I answered the phone on several occasions and told him she wasn't in. One night, I answered the phone, and here was this guy again asking the same question. Then to my surprise, he asked, "Well, what is your name?" I finally told him and then hung up. Then he started calling and asking for me.

During this rebound from Hunter, I didn't know how dangerous the situation was. Sean and I talked for weeks over the phone. Then one night, he asked to walk me to the campus library. It seemed harmless enough. He was older than me, tall and handsome in a certain way, with a nice smile and heavy voice. He also suffered with asthma. I enjoyed our date to the library and back to the dorm. I actually laughed and felt at ease with him. But it was a bittersweet feeling.

He listened and smiled as I shared my feelings about Hunter. He said, "Any guy that would leave a fine woman like you to go way across the country to play ball is crazy." Of course, I liked hearing that.

Sean called daily, and I looked forward to his calls. In my depressed, rebound mind, I slowly covered the pain in my heart for Hunter with my new feelings for Sean. We continued to see each other as we declared our feelings. Somehow, I truly believed that Hunter and I were through since I hadn't heard from him in months.

Finally, one night, Sean and I went out to dinner and later, in my foolish depressed state, we ended up in a cozy, little motel room—intimately. I felt close to this man, but somehow, it was a bittersweet relationship. A part of me cried out, "Where are you, Hunter? Help me! I need you." Sean nurtured a pain in my lonely heart, but I really desired that intimacy in marriage with Hunter. I still believed in the strict principles I had been taught at home, the little schoolhouse, and the little Baptist church.

Several weeks later, as Susan and I were in the dining hall, I became terribly ill. I wasn't sure what was going on. The following week, I had more discomfort and ended up in the Emergency Room. I immediately called Sean, and he came to the hospital. The doctor informed us that I was pregnant. Sean was calm, but I was frightened. He assured me that all would be well. From the kindness and gentleness he had shown me, I believed he would stand by me. So I thought!

We continued to see each other, and then I found myself asking, "Will we get married and give my baby a name and a home?" He always smiled, changed the subject, gave me a hug, and then became quiet.

Going through this, I thought of Hunter, but my mind could only handle one pressure at a time. After all, part of me believed we were through, and the other was either in denial or shock. I really believed Sean was going to marry me and be there for our baby. I needed someone to stand by their word for once and not disappoint me again. Most of all, I needed peace of mind. My mind was tired of juggling situations and trying to focus and survive. Finally, Sean said he couldn't make a permanent commitment now because of other obligations but that he did love me. I said, "What kind of obligations do you think I have?" He didn't answer, just dropped his head.

Sean continued to visit at the dorm and bring special foods for my new craving appetite. I looked forward to his visits. He took me to doctor appointments and waited patiently, though it took several hours. Despite his severe asthma, he still spent time with me. A part of me still cared for him. He had a heavy laugh that made me smile. I wanted him near, since I carried a part of him inside from our special relationship. He was there when I needed comfort for my wounded heart. His kindness was genuine but carried no commitments. It weighed little for what was ahead for me and my baby.

When the doctor announced my pregnancy at the hospital, Susan became quiet and withdrawn. She didn't speak all the way back to campus.

After Sean left, she came to my room and finally spoke. She was upset and crying. The first thing she said was, "How could you do this to Hunter?" I tried to explain that he and I had split up over three months ago, but she wouldn't listen. She kept crying and left my room in tears. I saw my little sister walk across the campus alone in tears. We had been together from the beginning and shared so much. Now my immature choices had divided us. Even my roommate gave me the third degree.

Suddenly, I felt very alone, alienated from my own sister and roommate. What had I done? A part of me wanted to stand on a hill and say, "Listen, everyone, I need your help! I am imprisoned and can't get out! This is how I got here. Help me! Don't judge me. I want to do the right thing. I just want to be loved and taken care of." In spite of it all, there was someone inside me very alive, which kept me going—my precious unborn baby.

Even though Susan was upset, I kept moving for my sanity and the unpredictable future of my child. Day after day, I tried to focus on my classwork and my situation. But it was very hard. I felt trapped between a rock and hard place.

I still had classwork to do for my instructors, and I was gaining weight. I still couldn't tell Mama and Daddy. So I just put it off as long as I could.

Susan finally started talking to me. I needed her so much. I think she and I both were afraid of what was coming, that one day I would have to leave her. We had agreed we would go through college and graduate together. Now with a baby on the way, I would eventually have to go home and make a life for us, and she would be alone. We would be separated. Every time I looked at her, my heart broke all over again.

My other challenge was PE class. We agreed that I couldn't continue the strenuous PE activities in my condition. I had to talk to our PE teacher and hope she would understand and help in some way.

One day after class, we went to her office, and I shared my sad story in tears. She was very compassionate and kind. She formulated a plan to help maintain my grades through less strenuous PE activities and extra homework. All my friends in PE looked out for me. I thank God for the grace He shared through my PE teacher, friends, and also my sister, who, I believed, finally forgave me.

It was during the winter of 1971 that Cora came for a visit. I shared my situation, and she assured me she'd soften the announcement to our parents. She had the type of personality to calm a storm with much ingenuity.

Susan and I went home for Christmas break, December of 1971, and I was really nervous. Sean and I were still seeing each other, but there was no discussion about marriage. I believed that it would solve all my problems. However, marriage to Sean was not in God's plan. Sean said he would stand by me and the baby. At the time, that was enough.

My biggest problem was dealing with my parents. While we were home, I stayed out of their sight constantly. Because they had borne so many children, it wouldn't be hard to see my symptoms and condition. Cora continually ran interference to shield me.

One evening while several of us were sitting by the fireplace, I became very nauseated. I was weaving back and forth behind Mama's chair while combing her hair. I gave some excuse, and Cora noticed my dilemma and took over. I went to the bedroom and crashed. I counted the days when we could return to school.

When we arrived back on campus, I sighed a big relief. I thought I had gotten away with it for a while, hoping to buy some time, until Sean decided to do the right thing.

In January 1972, our brother Tim and his wife decided to celebrate his birthday. He asked us to come and invite some of our friends from school.

By this time, I had gained more weight, and most of the friends on our floor knew my condition but were still supportive.

Cora came up with a great idea, or so we thought at the time. We'd invite Sean and our friends to the party, then go by our house and introduce my parents to Sean. While everyone was getting to know each other, she would gently break the news about my pregnancy.

We went along with the idea and invited our friends to meet our parents. Cora really dressed up the conversation, using herself as an example. Sean hastily spoke up and said he would do the right thing by me and the baby but never mentioned marriage.

Then I looked at my parents. Daddy dropped his head, and Mama just shook hers. We didn't give them a chance to speak or respond. We were out of there like a flash of lightning. That was so cruel. I was afraid and a coward.

We rushed over to my brother's party, so naïve, so foolish, not knowing how I'd hurt them and would need their support and help very soon.

At the party, we foolishly celebrated the announcement to my parents and Tim's birthday. In my mind, I was bittersweet happy.

I still had some support from Sean, but I couldn't get my parents' defeated look out of my mind.

Suddenly, I felt afraid for the future. Now look what I had done! We danced, ate, and played games at the party; and Cora assured me all would be well. I took little thought of tomorrow. My mind was tired of juggling events and trying to survive. Now for just a few hours, I rested and imagined all would be well. Sean held me close as we danced, and I laid my head on his shoulders and cried. A feeling came over me that much adversity was ahead and Sean wouldn't be there to help.

Cora returned to Michigan the following week. We wouldn't see her again for many years. After the party, we went back to the dorm, not stopping to think, perhaps our parents needed some consideration. I was so ashamed how I had hurt them. In my mind, I had to keep moving or collapse under the pressure. Even though we managed to tell them, I had no idea the long toilsome journey that awaited me and my precious baby.

Mama called from her job the following day. She was bitterly angry and yelled about how we laid the news on them and just left. I didn't blame her at all. I told her I was so sorry, but that was all I could do at the time. She continued and then eventually hung up.

I was left in shock because I finally realized how much I had wounded my parents. I wanted to tell them how the pain, hurt, and humiliation had started and this was the result. I wanted them to know I had been mentally and emotionally sick for some time, since the wedding was cancelled, that my life was on rebound and had started a precious new life; and that my vision had always been to get an education and make them proud.

Now I was another unwed mother statistic. But I wanted them to know I was scared about my survival and care of my baby. I also wanted to thank them for trying to help my depressed state by sending me to Michigan, but instead of healing, I had deep scars that have not healed. But all was not lost. I was still their daughter, and the principles that carried us through childhood saved me in that strange city. Through their training, I said no to things that could have cost my life; and they would not have seen me again, also, I needed them now more than ever, not the anger, not the judging but someone to understand. I was deeply depressed and wasn't far from a mental breakdown. I wanted to scream and say, "Mama, Daddy, help me. This is too hard! I need you! Don't you understand?"

After Mama hung up, I managed to refocus and prepare for class. I didn't know where I was going, but somehow, I knew there was a survival element in me that said, "Keep moving," and somehow I did. It was my precious baby. That no matter how lonely I felt, I carried someone who would be with me for nine long months, and I could tell him, "I love you and will never leave you."

Later that evening, I had another surprise. It was Hunter's sister.

She lived in the same dorm but on a different floor. We saw each other occasionally on campus but spoke briefly. We never stopped and talked about her brother. I don't know if he had told her about our breakup.

One night, she rushed up to my room and said Hunter was on the phone and wanted to talk to me. What do you think I did? In my unstable state, I rushed to her floor and picked up the phone as if nothing had happened. We had not talked for almost four months.

We confessed our love for each other and that we didn't mean to call our relationship off. He anxiously said his coach agreed we could get married. Now I could go to school out West with him.

As my heart leaped for joy at this news, I was quickly reminded of my condition. Then I angrily told him that I couldn't come because I was pregnant. "You left me here, and now I can't come."

He began shouting, wanting to know who it was and when it happened. At that moment, he forgot we had called it quits. I started to cry, and then he assured me it was going to be all right; that he would talk to his coach, and we would get married, and he would help care for my baby.

I went back upstairs to my room more confused than ever but thinking that maybe I would finally have my intended husband after all, even with all the challenges of our lives. Sean couldn't make a commitment. Maybe now, carrying another man's child, Hunter was ready to demonstrate his love and commitment to me.

As fate would have it, I had more complications, resulting in admission to the campus clinic. The strain of my situation was affecting me physically, and my immune system was in chaos. Sean came to see me but still no solutions. I didn't hear from Hunter anymore.

One Sunday, my parents showed up at the infirmary after church. Susan had told them I was ill. You'd think they'd be in a good Christian mood. Mama was on one side of my bed, giving me the third degree and Daddy on the other. They said I must leave school, come home, and have this baby before I lose it.

After the scolding, they assured me that things would work out but it wouldn't be easy. Then Daddy said, "I hope we have a fine grandson." I looked at him and turned my head to the side. I was so ashamed.

I agreed to leave college and go home. Mama said she would come back and take me home. When they left, I cried for them, myself, my baby, Hunter, and my sister whom I would leave behind, and Sean, whom I had grown so close to. As I was carrying his child, I suddenly realized that he wouldn't be a part of me and my baby's life.

Sean didn't come in the infirmary to face my parents. He was outside dodging. Maybe he was wise, because Mama may have beaten him with her pocketbook.

When I saw him, I knew it was over." His actions had indicated his interest was elsewhere, though he tried.. How sad, because in my heart I would have been a committed wife to him and our baby, despite my dormant feelings for Hunter.

I left college feeling I had attended a funeral and was going to another: to face my family and community. Everyone saw me as a traitor to Hunter. For many years after that, I allowed everyone to believe what they wanted, even though, I felt like a crucible. The only thing that kept me going was a little life that I had to protect and love and hope he never experience the pain I had.

It was so hard leaving Susan. Mama and my sister-in-law Sherry came to take me home. Susan left the car in tears. I cried too, dying inside. I had broken our chain. We had shared so much together. It seemed so unreal to see her return to the dorm. How would she make it alone?

But I had to go home and prepare for this new life.

I cried many nights for the pain I caused everyone, even myself, because so many people believed in me that I would finish college and be a fine teacher.

Through my tears, I reached out to the God, who had talked to me when I was a child, running around in the dark woods. I began to experience a peace that I never knew existed. This peace helped me understand that I must stop living in a dream world and face the consequences of my choices.

I begin to realize that despite what Hunter and Sean did or did not do, what I had done was wrong. I had disobeyed God by having a relationship outside of marriage, despite my mind-set. I had disobeyed him who had given His Son to die for my sins. Somehow, I wanted to make it right with the Lord before my precious baby was born. But how!

Suddenly, all my concerns shifted to the life I was carrying... No matter what happens, my baby wouldn't feel the rejection I had experienced. Secondly, maybe I shouldn't blame Hunter for not being there. Perhaps he was dealing with similar pressures. If he loved me like he said, he surely had experienced a broken heart also. He had always hoped we would get our education despite the disappointments we went through. Plus, his education was a great milestone for his family. Even though I don't know what happened with him out West, he was still a human being and deserved compassion. Maybe he wanted to do the right thing but struggled with the right decisions.

However, I vowed to be a devoted mother, even though I didn't have anything but a broken heart and love to offer my child. That must be enough for now.

In the spring of 1972, depressed, defeated, embarrassed, and deserted, I left college and my little sister and went home. It was time to prepare for the life I carried: the promise of a better day, even though I didn't know it at the time.

The ride home was long as we traveled in quietness. No one spoke, and I dared not. I looked at the highway that Susan and I had traveled many times from college to home. I looked at the trees that I loved to watch as the wind blew their branches. Now it seemed the wind stopped blowing and the branches bowed their head in silent sadness. Most of all, I feared facing the look on my father's face.

I didn't feel worthy to walk back into my parents' home. After all, the last time I was there, I had treated them so coldly, telling them the news and leaving without giving them a chance to respond. In a sense, the lesson I was learning was justified. I just needed my parents' mercy and most of all God's.

When I walked in our home and saw my father, I dropped my head in shame, just as he did. But Daddy compassionately said, "Hold your head up. You are my daughter." As he spoke in his gentle voice, I began to realize that my parents' love had been there all the time. I had been so distracted by my selfish interests.

Mom took good care of me. We visited needy families in the community, helping others and preparing for my baby. I felt really bad for my parents. In addition to our large family, Granddaddy was back with us, and to make room for me and a baby was a big challenge, but Mama worked it out.

As I began to renew my relationship with the Lord, I felt compelled to make things right at church.

One Sunday, the preacher made an appeal, and I walked courageously to the altar of our little church and rededicated my life to Christ. I wanted the Lord's anointing and favor on me and my baby. I asked for His forgiveness for my sins and not trusting Him. I also thanked Him for granting me the privilege, even through my unwise choices to mold a new life for Him. I knew the road would be long for us. But for the first time, I had an assurance that I was not alone. That Immanuel, God with us, was with me.

As I was going to the altar, I overhead a mother of the church, supposedly, one of my parents' friends, say, "What is she going up there for?" It hurt badly, but I kept walking. That Sunday, my personal relationship with the Lord was renewed.

It's so sad the damage church members cause to the weak. This mother should have nurtured and reassured me of God's love. Our people have a long way to go to model Christ.

God instilled in me a strength I never knew existed. Despite the fact I had made wrong choices, I had faith that God would help me raise this child. From that day forward, I kept walking and trusting. The more I walked, God's peace overshadowed me despite the challenging days ahead.

During the late spring of 1972, my mind began to settle that Hunter and Sean had their own concerns and I must face the future alone. My attention must be for my baby and rebuild my faith in God.

Much to my surprise, Hunter came for a visit on spring break from college. However, I wasn't home. I had gone to the hair dresser, and spent the night with Tim and his wife, Sherry.

That particular day, we were watching T.V. when suddenly we heard a car outside. Sherry went to the window and said, "Sal, guess who's outside, Hunter!" I wanted to die! I couldn't let him see me like this. So I rushed in her bedroom and locked the door. I couldn't, and wouldn't, face this six-foot-seven man that I supposedly had betrayed. That was the thought on everyone's mind. I heard it so much until I believed it myself. I decided if I stayed in that room long enough, maybe he would go away.

I heard his voice as he walked in the house and asked, "Where's Peach?" He knocked on the door several times and called my name. I was so ashamed to face him. My slim body was gone, and in its place was a fat little butterball, carrying another man's child. I asked God to grant me the courage to face him.

Finally, I came out of the room but couldn't look at him. I stood by the warm fireplace with my head down. He came over to me and said, "Peach, I still love you." Then I looked up at this tall giant and said, "Hunter, I still love you too." We hugged and spent most of the day walking and talking together. However, there was no discussion of taking me back with him. He did say he would be back in August when the baby comes.

While Hunter was home, he and Mama took me to my doctor appointments in Jackson.

One day, Mama decided to do some shopping before leaving Jackson. I stayed in the car as Hunter accompanied her in the store. Out of nowhere, Sean walked by, wearing a tennis outfit and carrying a tennis racket. He noticed me in the car and stopped and asked how I was doing. Then he gave me a little money to assist with my doctor bills and rushed off to his appointment. My heart was broken all over again. I didn't know Hunter was watching.

After he left, Hunter came back to the car and asked if he was the one. I said yes.

We all rode in silence back home. Oh Lord, when does it stop hurting? Hunter visited a few more times before he returned to school. He even went to church with us. He was hailed as a martyr and me as a betrayer by our family and church members. I pressed on. Somehow, a part of me died daily; but another part was saying, "You must survive. You will survive for your baby. God is with you. Oh, thank You, Immanuel!"

"Restore unto me the joy of thy salvation; and
Uphold me with thy free spirit.
Evening, and morning, and at noon, will I pray,
And cry aloud: and He shall hear my voice."

—Ps. 51:12; 55:17

Chapter 8

THE HOPE, A NEW BUD

The first week of August, Hunter returned home. I was comforted that he was here for me, though I knew it was difficult for him.

It was getting close to my delivery. As usual, I was in the kitchen making Granddaddy's favorite flapjacks, when I began to have contractions. Mama was working in Clinton. She had left explicit instructions if my labor started.

Sherry called Mama and Hunter. We picked them up and rode to the hospital. When we arrived, the doctor examined me and said, "The baby won't be here until late tonight." So they brought me home, packed my bag, and waited.

Sherry thought it best to wait at her parents' home, since they were closer to the hospital. After dinner, I lay in bed thinking about everything but was anxious to see my baby. I knew Hunter was dealing with a lot of emotions. It was very hard for us to talk to each other.

My pains got closer, and off to the hospital we went. Tim wasted no time getting us there. When we arrived, I vomited all over the ER. Then the nurse took me to labor and delivery. There was no time to say goodbye to anyone because I was in pain and so nauseous.

Later, there was a pain beyond imagination that my small body experienced to delivery my baby. A surgical procedure was also performed. The Lord blessed me with a son, a new bud, to add to the life of this battered rose, among the thorns, to restore my joy.

Terrance Leon Mack was born August 8, 1972, at 2:00 a.m. I had dozed off after the delivery, but Mama awakened me to see my baby, my son. He was the most beautiful baby I had ever seen. The pain, depression, and disappointment was worth it all when I looked at my precious little boy, who had survived inside me amidst my struggles, and pain. As a young twenty-year-old, inexperienced mother, I had carried him, not knowing what another day would bring but hopeful because I had something worth living, worth hoping, worth surviving for now. The joy of holding him, loving him made it worthwhile.

I was in pain and very weak from the delivery and surgery so I remained in the hospital until I could walk and move without aid. Still it was a joyful pain for the gift God had given to me. I was so thankful for my healthy baby.

However, my mind clouded with uncertainties. Though Hunter was home, I wanted to see Sean first. I wanted him to see what our special love that nurtured me in my loneliest and darkest moments had brought, a special little baby boy.

Sean didn't come to the hospital neither did Hunter. I called Sean's home several times, but no answer. Even if Sean didn't know our baby was here, where was Hunter? He knew where I was. He had brought me here.

While I was thinking about the two deserters, another unknown situation had occurred in the nursery. It was a miracle how God intervened through my mother. She came to see me every day.

One day, she came to the hospital and went straight to the nursery. When she came back, she looked troubled. I didn't have a private room. All the rooms were full, so my bed was in the hall with other unwed mothers and patients. I asked Mama what was wrong. Was the baby all right? She kept asking, "Do you remember what your baby looks like?" I said, "Yes, ma'am, but what is wrong?" She said, "Okay, I'll be back." She was gone for a long time, so I began to worry.

When she finally came back, she was carrying Lil T. She placed him in my arms and said, "Is this your baby?" I looked at him and said, "Yes, ma'am, this is my baby. Why did you ask?"

She finally said she didn't want to worry me. But when she went to the nursery earlier, someone had mistakenly placed Little T's name tag on another baby. When she looked at the other baby, she knew it wasn't T. When she told the nurses, they denied it. As she persisted, they changed the name tags and put Little T's tag back on him.

When she told me, I shuddered and held my baby close. To think they make mistakes like that in the nursery. Mama said, "Our baby is also prettier. We knew T's face because we had seen him after the delivery." Thank You, Lord, for Mama's wisdom. We later laughed about the incident. However, at the time, it wasn't funny at all.

When I left the hospital, I felt so alone. But I had my little boy, and I'd do whatever was necessary to keep him from feeling unwanted. I was numb with depression but determined to let Terrance know he was loved. I kept telling myself that God was with me, as I learned to lean on His promises instead of my emotions.

After being home a few days, Hunter showed up. He didn't say much. I didn't have much to say to him either. He sat in the chair, staring at me and Terrance. He did that on two visits, then got up and left.

I asked Mama what was wrong with him. She said he was trying to sort things out in his mind. The next time he came, he was preparing to return to school. He picked up Terrance and kissed him and said, "I wish you were my baby." I cried out, "Well, he's not your baby, and if you can't accept him, you can't accept me." Then in tears, we hugged, and he left. He said he would keep in touch with me and the baby and would return during winter break. In the back of my mind, I knew he wouldn't, but I stayed hopeful.

How I wanted to tell him "this baby could have been yours if you hadn't changed our future, if you loved me enough. But, I didn't want to be cruel. I knew he was carrying his own burdens.

God was slowly showing me that some things weren't in His plan and I must accept it.

The next time I saw Hunter, it was winter of 1972, when Terrance was six months old. He had aged and looked sad. He stopped by unexpectedly one night, and I was very upset with him. There had been no calls, nothing. I had heard rumors that he was home on several occasions, but he didn't come to see me.

For months, I had called, wrote, and sent quilts to keep him warm. When I did reach him by phone, he always appeared in a hurry or sounded ill. Maybe he was emotionally sick as I was. I don't know.

Week after week, I sat on our little country porch with T and looked down the long road that connected our home to the main highway. No Hunter! No Sean! Even the letters became less. I cried and grieved for him to come, but it didn't happen.

When I'd hear he was home, I'd dressed Terrance and myself in special outfits and wait. Some days, I walked the long road with Terrance singing, hoping to meet him. Then I'd take long walks along that same road alone and talk to God. I told Jesus about my broken dreams and how I wanted a better life for my son. That one day, if it took many years, I hoped to return to college and complete my education, and set an example for my son. I owed my baby that much. Oh Lord, help me!

One day, my heart hurt so badly I thought I was going to die and leave Terrance. That snapped me back to reality, that I must look to God for strength and love and not to man. Most of all, I must survive for my son.

That night, I knew it was over. I was very angry with him. One of my younger brothers was holding Terrance. He looked at him and turned away.

On the porch, we hugged for the last time. It would be thirty years before we'd see each other again. It was my way of saying, "You are released from this web. Go and fulfill your dream!" I already knew Sean was out of my life, so I didn't expect anything from him.

After Hunter left, I decided it was time to make a life for T and me. I was afraid. I hadn't heard from Sean to help with support. My working skills were limited, except some typing I had learned in high school.

Mama reminded me to apply for welfare, but I refused. Finally, I swallowed whatever pride I had left and applied for government assistance and anything else we were eligible for, because I needed help. However, I was not satisfied with welfare.

After T was a year old, I went job hunting. I took him everywhere with me. I wanted people to know I was serious about supporting my child and wasn't another welfare case. Mama wanted to care for him while I job hunted, but I needed his closeness to keep me going. He and my faith made life worth living, and provided the courage to face the challenges ahead.

Whatever I was living for was solely for him. I prayed and cried often for this new life. Somehow, I knew God had not deserted me. I just didn't know how it would work out. Daily, I looked in his little face and said, "I love you," and held him close. He was a joy to love.

To get to the job interviews, I used a bus service that took prospective employees to job interviews and health centers for appointments. Twice a week, I got up, dressed T, packed his things, and rode the bus to the interviews. The employers thought it unusual for a woman to bring a child to an interview, but they said, "You are a very conscientious mother."

I was blessed to meet a nice social worker, who helped in my job search and offered words of encouragement, for my depressed spirit. He scheduled interview appointments until I was finally hired. He fed and played with T as I completed the applications. I thank and bless God for his kindness to T and me.

By God's grace, I was hired as a medical transcriber at the comprehensive health center in Jackson. I didn't have a clue what I was doing, but my supervisor gave me a chance. I received limited training and a large medical dictionary to interpret the medical records. It helped little, as I struggled with this new job.

However, being a former spelling bee champ helped considerably. Mom always said, "Do your best, child, and try to learn fast." Finally, I was transferred to another department making embossed medical cards and keeping records. I liked that better.

One day, my cousin in Jackson said he had seen Sean. Susan also saw him on campus with other girls. She got so angry talking about him. I told her it was okay. I have my little T. He was not hurting for anything. He was a beautiful child, rarely cried, except when he was hungry. He had a deep voice and was asthmatic like Sean. We spent many hours at the doctor with his condition. It did make my heart sick to hear Sean's name. A part of me wanted him to see his son, and another wanted to strangle him for deserting us.

One night, he showed up at our home, unannounced to see T. T looked much like him with the ears and mouth. I was hesitant at first but agreed.

He commented on how fine a baby he was. He promised to do much for T but fulfilled very little. Still, I permitted him to see T whenever he asked. He came back into our life for a brief time. He took me to work and introduced me and T to his mother and sister. They were so happy to see him. Our relationship didn't go very well after that, because he was still so unsettled and uncommitted. I needed someone in my life and T's to make a commitment or none at all.

God continued to work and open doors for us.

It was during my transfer to this new department that I met a very special lady, my supervisor, Mrs. Sharon Goins. She was always kind and thoughtful. Often, Mama sent Ms. Goins samples of her delicious country cooking.

One day, she asked if I would consider a school and work opportunity in Knoxville, Tennessee, to help support us. It would mean leaving T temporarily with my parents until I got settled with a job, housing, and find day care for Terrance.

Before she could finish, I blurted out, "No way, Ms. Goins! No! I will not leave my baby. I know what it's like to be left alone and deserted, and I won't do that to my baby. He and my little faith in God is all I have. I won't leave my child. Please don't ask me to do that. I won't! I won't!"

Just the thought of leaving him reminded me of the painful experiences of the past. I couldn't do that to my little boy, as I cried and continued to listen.

Mrs. Goins had become like a mother in my life, and she understood my hesitancy to her offer. When she learned about Sean and met him, she cautioned me that I could easily be locked in a future, without a vision, no commitments, and no responsibility. Did I want that for me and my child?

Night after night, I pondered her suggestion and thought to myself, "I just can't leave my child." Still I knew a decision had to be made about our future, even if it meant a sacrifice. When I think about it now, it reminds me of the sacrifice that God made, sending His Son, Jesus Christ, to die for the sins of the world. I must sacrifice the time from Terrance in order to secure a decent future for us. I tearfully prayed for guidance.

A week later, she brought the subject up again. My response was, "How can I leave Little T?"

As she comforted me, she tearfully looked in my eyes and said, "Georgia, you must be strong. I see a special strength in you. God is with you. He has a special plan for your life. I don't know what it is. But stand on your faith that has carried you this far. You've got to do this for you and Terry, as she called him. There is no vision for you in Bolton but a repeat of what you are going through. Terry deserves the best of you. I have seen you with him and know how much you love this child. Have faith in the God you talk about. Now is the time. Your parents will take good care of him. You should know that by now. They've been there with you all the way with Terry."

Days later, as I looked at my situation, I knew I had to charter the unknown for us to have a decent life. Mom and Dad had done all they could. They even rearranged the furniture and gave up their large bedroom so T and I could have our space. They took a smaller room in the house. That was love. Now with God's help, I had to strike out on my own.

The next day at work, I painfully said yes to Mrs. Goins and yes to leaving my baby behind. She contacted her friend at Knoxville College to make arrangements for my travel, lodging and the new job and school opportunity.

I counted the days before I had to leave. I held on to Terrance daily like glue, as if I wouldn't see him again. I walked and talked to my little boy and told him over and over again, "Mama is going away for a little while to make a future for us. I don't want to go. I don't want to leave you. But I have to if we are going to have a decent future. But I promise you, I will be back. Mama wants you to be a big boy. Granny and Granddaddy will take good care of you. Aunt Susan will be home from college to care for you also." He looked at me with his large, beautiful eyes as if to say, "Why are you crying, Mama?" As I talked with him, I cried and asked the Lord to give me strength.

As my departure drew near, I watched over him like an angel when he slept.

When he awoke and cried, I hurriedly picked him up, knowing that one day he would cry for me and I wouldn't be there. He would look for me with those large sad eyes, and I would be far away but, oh, for just a little while. Help me, Lord. This is too hard!

The day before I left, Ms. Goins invited my parents, T, and me to her home for dinner and to help with items for the trip. Mama kept asking her, "Now tell me again how things are going to be with Georgia Ann in Knoxville?" Mama was hurting as much as I was. She and Daddy had seen me through struggles from the beginning and had loved and nurtured T. They felt my pain and disappointments but didn't know all the things to say at the time but kept reminding me, "The Lord will provide. He will make a way somehow. Just trust Him!"

"Hear my cry, O God; attend unto my prayer. From the ends off the earth will I cry unto thee, when my heart is overwhelmed: lead me to the rock that is higher than I. For thou hast been a shelter for me, and a strong tower from the enemy."

—*Ps. 61:1–3*

Chapter 9

THE JOURNEY OF FAITH

It was May of 1974 when I accepted the job in Knoxville, Tennessee. T was eighteen months old. It was the hardest thing I've ever done, leaving my baby. It hurt more because T was asleep when I left. Tim, his friend, and their wives drove me to Knoxville. I cried all the way. I wanted them to stop the car and let me out. That part of me and my faith had carried me, and now I was leaving, almost deserting him. What more could my heart take?

I knew my parents would take good care of him. I never doubted that. I just wanted him with me. I wanted to say again, "Remember our little talk, Mommy will be back." Of course, Mama and I knew if I woke him, I would never leave. If he had suddenly woke up and cried for me, I would not have left.

Little T was a good baby and rarely cried, even when he was hungry. The thought of him waking up, looking for me pierced my heart like a sword. As I reflect now, perhaps it was my first commission from Christ (Matt. 28:18–20) to go and make a life for you and T saying, "Go and I will be with you." Mama always reminded me, "The Lord never puts more on us than we can bear."

However, that day, it felt unbearable. Today, my heart still aches when I recall life consequences that separated us for a season.

On August 8, 2019, Terrance turned forty-seven years old. We talked from Virginia to Tennessee and reminisced on past years. He couldn't see my tears, but I know he felt it in my voice.

I didn't understand the whys and hows, but I know now at age sixty-seven the God I serve is faithful. I challenge every reader of this book to surrender your life to him. Whatever challenges are before you, keep trusting even when you can't see, because it's not a seeing thing, it is a faith thing. If we just hold on, we will see, "This I recall to my mind, therefore I have hope. It is of the Lord's mercies that we are not consumed, because His compassions fail not. They are new every morning: Great is thy faithfulness. The Lord is my portion, saith my soul; therefore will I hope in him" (Lam. 3:21–24).

Oh Lord, life consequences are so strange. May we never forget there is a God leading our lives, who understands our grief and sorrows and loves us endlessly. Though he respects our choices and permits us to go through challenges, he has promised never to leave or forsake us. No one but an all-wise God and Savior could work the miracles He wrought in T and my life. Thank You, Lord.

The trip to Knoxville seemed endless. I had never traveled that distance in a car. When we passed the exit for Knoxville, Alabama, we thought we were there but only halfway. That only added to the pain. Every mile reminded me of my precious little boy, my heart I had left behind. What frightened me was what if I never saw my baby again?

We arrived late that evening at Knoxville College. We were met by the financial aid director, my new supervisor. He showered us with hospitality in his home and provided overnight lodging.

The next morning, my brother and company left for Mississippi. I felt so alone. I was left in an unknown place—to charter an unknown course without my baby and them. I sent what was left of my aching heart back to little T. I stood on Knoxville College campus, looking around at this new place as my brother drove off. What awaited me in this strange city? I had been in a strange city before. I told myself, "Oh, Lord, let me focus. Help me get settled quickly so I can go back and get my baby. Please, Lord, help me make better choices. Thank you for T, to live, work and survive for, and my renewed faith in you."

I became settled, working at the college and residing in the Towers, the tallest building on campus. I counted the days when I could leave and get my son. Every night, I cried myself to sleep because I didn't have my baby to hold for comfort. I tried to learn my job as quick as possible, but sometimes it was hard to concentrate.

My clerical duties included processing award letters and delivering mail to the dorms after work. Many students came into the office, especially the football players. I greeted them but found it hard to smile. I had not smiled for three years, only when I held T. Some of the guys tried to initiate a conversation, but I found it hard to respond. If anyone showed an interest in me, I immediately put up my guard. I didn't trust a man with my heart.

One day, a football player, wearing a big smile and covered with mud, came into the office. He greeted me, but I gave little attention, only the information he requested. He was from Fort Meade, Florida, near Tampa. His name was Dave Willis Shingles. He returned the next day, handsomely dressed and smiled. He sat by my desk and looked into my eyes. I indicated that if it wasn't about financial aid, I couldn't talk with him. So he smiled and left. However, he returned two days later. He said he liked me and wanted to take me on a date. I told him I wasn't interested, so he respected my wishes and left.

One evening while delivering the mail, someone called, "Hello, beautiful lady." I kept walking, barely looking up. It was that football player, riding in a car with his friend. The next evening, the same thing occurred. He got out the car, smiling, and offered to carry the mail. But I said no. I also noticed a serious limp when he walked. I asked him what was wrong with his leg. He said he had hurt it playing football.

The next day, he invited me to a movie on campus entitled *The Autobiography of Ms. Jane Pittman*. I said, "No, thanks." Then he started calling me after work. I finally told him, "Please leave me alone. I don't want to be bothered."

The following week, he called again, asking me to the movie. I finally said yes. After the movie, we walked around the campus and talked. He said he was from Fort Meade, Florida, on a football scholarship, and his vision was to play professional football. I'd always thought football players were loud and rude. However, his demeanor was kind and gentle in a special way, and I felt a little at ease with him. Everyone liked him, and his football name was "Black Juice."

One day, he came by the office while my supervisor was away. He sat near my desk, looked into my eyes, and asked why I was so sad. I hesitated. Then, sensing his concern, I tearfully began sharing my sad story.

He sat and listened for an hour as I worked and talked about my son. He came back the next day and walked me home. I told him I was reluctant to talk to men, because I carried a broken heart and it had not healed and I missed my son terribly. As I cried, he put his arms around me and comforted me. He was still walking with a limp. As I continued to inquire about his injury, he reluctantly went to the infirmary. The nurse put a support brace on his leg to help him walk. I learned from my coworkers that he was one of the college's fastest running backs but was injury prone. He would play at any cost, even injured, but was known as one of the nicest guys on campus.

Slowly, I began to think if a guy would sit and listen to my sad story and encourage me, maybe he did care. Still I didn't want to take a chance. I had to stay focused for my son. He continually tried to comfort my broken heart and focus my mind on the future. However, my only vision was to get my son and hold him, never letting him go.

One night after walking around the campus, we sat on the white concrete bench in front of the administration building. I talked and cried, as he listened. The pain and heartache of the past still overwhelmed me. The scars were so deep. I was afraid that something would happen, and I wouldn't see my little boy again. Then he put his arms around me and comforted me in a way I hadn't felt in a long time. Then we kissed. It felt like a kiss of hope. I thought that maybe my heart was beginning to heal. Still, I was reluctant to let him get too close.

When it was time to return home for T, he offered to purchase my bus ticket. I was very thankful.

As I boarded the bus, I cried for joy and sadness to hold my son again. I put Dave out of my mind. I just wanted to think of my son and hold him. Anything that was happening with Dave and me had to wait. T was my first priority. Anyway, this could be another guy with false hopes.

I returned home in the fall of 1974 to get T. I counted the hours when the bus would arrive in Jackson, and I would hold my little boy in my arms again. When I saw him, he had changed. He was so big. They had cut his hair, and he looked so handsome. When he saw me, he cried, and so did I. Hearing his deep cry, I rushed and took him in my arms.

I told him how much I loved him and that I would never leave him again. We clung to each other, fearing we would be separated again. I was so thankful to my parents and sister Susan for taking care of my son.

Susan was also getting married, and I was in her wedding. Dave called and asked if he could come to meet my family. My parents also wanted to meet him. They didn't want me to get hurt again, and they were very protective of T.

I assured them we were taking things slow, and he was kind to me. My sister's wedding was very nice. However, it opened up old wounds, reminding me what I missed three years ago with Hunter. When I was alone, I cried and asked God to soothe my painful heart and help me forget the pain and take care of my baby. After the wedding and reception, we returned to Knoxville. I was content to leave because Mississippi was full of so many sad memories. Everything there, reminded me of Hunter and the times we spent together. Mama and Daddy were so attached to T they didn't want him to go. But I wasn't leaving without my son. We both had endured much being apart. Dave also helped me drive my Chevy Malibu back to Knoxville.

T's babysitter was Ms. Thomas. She and her husband picked T up in the morning and brought him home at night. They were a big help to me. I counted the hours when I'd get off work and see my son. However, he suffered from asthma. Whenever he had a high temperature, I'd rush him to the doctor.

One afternoon when I tried to wake him, he was burning up with a fever. His face had turned red. We rushed him to the ER where he was diagnosed with pneumonia. I thanked the Lord for sparing his life. With care and medication, we nursed him back to health. I included T in my entire schedule when I wasn't at work.

91

Dave dressed him in a cute little tuxedo and we took him to his football banquet. He and I were also in the Knoxville College 1974 Homecoming parade.

Residing on Knoxville College campus provided an opportunity to attend class, work, and care for my son.

After working in the financial aid office for several months, I transferred to the Cooperative Education Department. Dave was getting even closer to us. He and T loved spending time together. I was somewhat happy but not thrilled. Should I trust him with my little boy and with my heart that hadn't healed? I watched him carefully. As he, T, and I spent time together; I began to believe that he was a blessing.

Often we'd sat on the grassy hill in front of the Towers and watch Dave practice. Mama called often to check on us and my relationship with this new man. She was content to hear how T and Dave were getting along. Still, she had misgivings.

We continued to date and grew closer. Dave became a compassionate and nurturing figure in me and my son's life. Slowly, I began to return his love and believe that I could trust someone else with my heart.

He was always looking out for Terrance. If the day care driver was late bringing him home, he worried. He and T was a special team. Dave carried him around campus, always holding his hand and T looking up at him with large joyful eyes. That made me happy. As time passed, my feelings continued to grow for this new man in my life.

In the fall of 1975, we were married in the small Baptist church T and I attended. Dave, T, and I became a family. My mother attended the wedding and gave us her ring and blessings, though still a little reserved with my new husband, because she knew my heart had not completely healed.

Dave was now a husband, football player, student, and worked part-time at UPS. I was working in the Cooperative Education Department. Dave and I adjusted to our new life together, though I stayed depressed from time to time.

Working full-time and going to school took a toll on my frail body. I never gained the weight I lost the summer of 1970. I suffered from depression, anemia, and tension in my back. I enjoyed taking care of T. I worried that Dave had so much responsibility, so I worked hard to be a good wife and mother to take some of the load off him. As we continued our new life together – my job closed due to budget cuts. I was so disappointed! However, the unemployment benefits and Mama's training was a blessing.

*"Come and hear, all ye that fear God, and I will
declare what He hath done for my
soul."*

—*Ps. 66:16*

Chapter 10

The Enduring Family

In the spring of 1976, We were blessed with a beautiful baby boy, Dave Willis Shingles Jr., fondly DJ. The labor and delivery was hard, but it was worth it all. He had deep dimples that took the nurses' breath away, and he looked like Dave. Terrance was so happy to have a little brother to play with and help care for. By this time, we had moved from the Towers to the College Hills Apartments on Western Avenue, right down from the college.

I continued to draw unemployment and care for our two boys. I also learned that "God works in mysterious ways, His wonders to perform." While at home, I had special time with T and our new baby.

One day, I noticed something unusual about DJ's foot. Usually a baby's foot will grow into shape after several months following birth. Not with DJ. His right foot looked like a golf club. I called my friends and cried over the phone, that something was wrong with my baby. They came by and referred me to a foot specialist, who confirmed our fears.

Adjustments had to be done promptly for him to walk correctly while his bones were still soft.

His leg and foot would be placed in a cast for several months. He would wear special orthopedic shoes with the toes out to keep the leg and foot straight. If we didn't do it now, he would be crippled.

We prayed for guidance and agreed to the procedure. When they turned his foot, he cried in anguish, so did I. When it was over,

I held him close and reassured him it was okay. It took a long time before he stopped crying. We prayed as he wore the cast, hoping it would straighten his foot.

DJ was irritable the whole time. When the cast finally came off, we were so happy. However, the little saw they used scratched his leg, leaving a scar that has almost disappeared today. He wore the special shoes for several months and finally graduated to regular baby shoes.

As he began to walk, we thanked the Lord that his foot was straight. I thought of and prayed for other mothers who experienced our trauma and worse situations. Sometimes now when we are visiting, I observe his walk and remember that special time God was our Great Physician for DJ.

As one of the fastest running backs at KC, Dave was chosen to play in a special football game in California. He was on the West Team of Small Colleges All American. We were able to see him on television. The boys and I missed him terribly. We didn't have any other family members in Knoxville. It was the four of us and a few close friends from the college and the Baptist church family.

The pressures of trying to work, play ball, be a husband and student took an additional toll on our marriage. He continued to get injured on the field but still hoped for a career in professional football. However, that didn't happen.

I prayed for years that our family and God's purpose for him would fill that part of his life. Even now when he is watching a football game, I can see that unfilled vision in his eyes. However, I reassured him that God had something better, like building a strong family for Christ's kingdom. He always answers, "Yes, dear, you are right."

In the spring of 1980, God blessed us with a beautiful little girl, born on Dave's birthday. We were all surprised. We call her our little princess even to this day. She had a gleam in her eye that seemed to say, "I've got things to do. So let's get on with this baby scene." As the only girl and born on her daddy's birthday, she was a joy to Dave, myself, and her brothers.

Dave was working at the Baptist Hospital and taking apprentice electrician classes at night. We were living on Washington Avenue and struggling to pay our bills.

However, during my pregnancy, I was sickly, anemic, and frail, and suffered from a depressed spirit. I worked as an insurance claims representative. I liked my job and coworkers, but I was sick all the time. I also carried a special cup because I kept spitting up this extra saliva, which was typical with all my pregnancies. Mama suspected that I was carrying a girl because of my symptoms. She convinced Dave to bring me and the boys to live with her until I was stronger.

Even though I was married to a special man and loved him dearly, the memories of the past continually resurfaced. I didn't want to be away from Dave, but the doctor recommended physical and mental rest. So I agreed to go.

When we traveled to Mississippi, I relived the past. Seemed like every mile from Knoxville to Bolton reminded me that, I was returning to memories of pain. With a weak immune system and a depressed spirit, I worried that being in Mississippi would be so overwhelming, it might endanger my carrying this child, But I had to trust God and go, and know that the same God who had carried me in the past was present now. Mama took good care of me and the boys and took me to doctor appointments, but my spirit stayed low.

During my stay in Mississippi, Sean learned we were home and asked to see Terrance. I was reluctant, but Mama and Dave said, "Let him come so he can't say you kept him from seeing his son." I knew seeing him would open up old wounds. But I put my feelings aside and agreed.

T was seven years old now, handsome, and tall for his age. He had not seen Sean for several years. However, when I introduced him to Sean again, he smiled and then looked shyly away. T was friendly with him but looked to Dave as his father. He was looking more like Sean as he got older. Sean still shared false hopes for T and fulfilled none.

The next time he asked to see T, I was preparing to take him to the doctor for an asthma attack. When he offered to take us, I reluctantly agreed, since I was still weak.

It was painful to look in the eyes of my son's biological father, who had nurtured and deserted me. Anything I felt for him was gone. T seemed glad to see him. I swallowed my pride and for T's sake permitted him to spend some time with him.

Weeks later, Dave came to take us home. We were glad to see him. He was lonely and wanted us with him. However, Mama wasn't ready to let us go. He stayed about a week, and we returned home with goodies from Mama's house.

Being with Dave gave me a healing comfort. As we drove back to Knoxville, I looked back quickly and tearfully said farewell to the sad memories. My mind could rest again. Back with my husband and our two boys, I felt strengthened as we looked forward to the arrival of our new baby, Ms. Kristie Danielle Shingles.

It was a crucial time for us financially in 1981. Dave was continually laid off from the electrical trade, and we had little money to support our family.

We were living on Washington Avenue, and the landlord refused to repair the house. The kitchen located in the rear had collapsed on the ground and were constantly overrun with field rats from the alley. We stayed up nightly watching and praying over our children and cleaning and disinfecting the house daily until we were exhausted.

Dave spoke with his boss, and he offered us an old duplex building, which wasn't much better. When he showed me the place, I said, "No way, my children and I will not stay in this place." It resembled an old storefront building that had been deserted. How could I live there with my children and bring a new baby there? Dave pleaded with me to move in until he could find something better.

With tearstained cheeks, I swallowed my pride and followed my husband. We also had given our notice to move and didn't have time or money to look elsewhere.

We cleaned and worked in the duplex until we were exhausted. We painted and did all we could to make it livable. Still it looked bad on the outside. I was ashamed for my friends and coworkers to know where I lived. I was very foolish and naïve. In my prideful state, I had forgotten that Mama often reminded us that, "Home is made on the inside with your values and principles, not what appears on the outside to please people. Godly principles with cleanliness and order is important."

I was also pregnant again and very afraid. Kristie was barely a year old. The doctor had informed us that carrying another baby due to my weak, anemic body may result in a miscarriage. Mama was also worried but turned our anxieties into trust and laughter. She reminded me that God will provide the strength to carry this baby.

When I tearfully shared the news of my pregnancy with Mama, she changed my outlook with her usual humor. She finally said, "Listen, that baby was up in heaven playing with Jesus when you and Dave said, 'Come on down.'" Suddenly, I stopped crying and started laughing. She assured me that God would provide.

One day, on the way from a workshop, I tearfully confided in a dear friend, a coworker. She reached over and took my hand and said, "You are not alone." That also lifted and restored my faith in God. Today, in outreach ministry, I can reach out to many and say, "You are not alone." I am here for you as God provided someone for me."

Near the end of my pregnancy, the obstetrician delivered Kenny a week earlier due to a small tear in my womb resulting in a longer stay in the hospital. Dave and our close friends took good care of the children while I was hospitalized.

Later, I went home with a beautiful, healthy baby. I always wanted twins, and this time I got the experience. I was breastfeeding Kenny, and Kristie was on the bottle. It was quite a handful. But God supplied the strength.

When my friend brought Kristie home, she walked into the house like she was on a mission. When she saw Kenny in her baby bed, she let out a scream that woke our neighbors. We tried to comfort her but to no avail. She didn't understand another baby taking her place. Dave tried to quiet her by walking outside, but she didn't want to be away from me. She cried so long the neighbors asked what was ailing her.

Dave told them we had a new baby, and she was upset.

Finally, Dave brought her to me. I was still weak from the delivery but found the strength to hold my two babies in my arms. I told her that Kenny was her baby, too, and that I needed her help to care for him. When I finished speaking, she calmed down and laid her head on my breast. Tears rolled down my face as I said, "Lord, grant me the strength to care for two babies. I didn't realize it at the time, but He had already put his promise in place, that "as our days, so shalt thy strength be" (Deut. 33:25).

The three of us finally fell asleep in my bed, as I held Kenny on one side and Kristie on the other.

Kristie and Kenny became best friends as they grew up together. She always looked out for him. They share their hopes, dreams and visions, reminding one another how God works in their lives.

God provided just as Mama said.

Times were hard, and trying to clothe another child was even harder. However, "God works in mysterious ways, His wonders to perform." God moved on a neighbor's heart to give name-brand clothes to Ken, for the first four years of his life. On many occasions we'd find a bag or box of items for the children left on our doorstep, reminding us that we were not alone. I praised and thank God, calling Mama and thanking her for the prayers and encouragement.

Little did I realize that God was putting us in position in that new neighborhood to receive a bountiful blessing beyond our imagination. Our new landlord refused to repair the place, plus an old semitractor was sitting in the backyard, adjacent to the electric company, owned by Dave's boss. Daily, it reminded me of our poor, pitiful state. Even with the Christian home we had established for our children, I worried that the neighbors saw us as outcasts. I was still very naïve.

If our family talked about visiting, I made excuses.

Daily, I looked out the kitchen window, praying for a better place for our family. Strangely, how my eyes kept resting on a house across the street. I wondered who lived there. I didn't know what that meant. I never saw anyone coming or going. The house seemed so lonely, just there in silence, so it seemed. I'd continue to gaze, then turn away and focus back on my present situation.

Because the new place was a duplex, the rent was high. We struggled four years there and met new friends in the community.

The families and schools respected us for the values we were instilling in the children. It became a witness to the community – that children reared in the inner city (with a vision) can become productive citizens.

My advice to others; utilized your circumstances and environment as tools to shine for Christ, not as hindrances to success. We prayed that our family would remember that.

God brought another special lady in the community into our lives, who also shared and help provide for the children. She reminded me of Mama, sharing food and clothing for our struggling family. Her name was Mrs. McMahan. She complimented me on our children's cleanliness and her admiration for my clothesline.

If we weren't home, Mrs. McMahan left items at the door with a note. She and I became dear friends. I loved her as the mother I was missing back home. Whenever I thanked her, she said it wasn't necessary. However, it meant more than she would ever know.

When we moved to a new place, I returned and visited her on many occasions. Soon she began to experience health challenges.

One day, I shared how much her friendship meant to our family and that without her, we wouldn't have made it. God had planted her in our lives for a special reason. We hugged and cried, and I told her I would never forget her, that I loved her dearly!

When she passed, our neighborhood wasn't the same. Even today, when I pass her home, my heart longs to see her sitting on the porch swing and to hear her voice. I cry inside for my own mother, who is asleep in Christ. Oh, how I miss you, Mama, and you Mrs. McMahan.

I say to everyone, cherish your mother while you have her. When she is gone, only Jesus can mend your broken heart.

In 1985, Dave was hired by the IBEW local union to work out of state as a journeyman/electrician.

Work was plentiful on the road but scarce here, especially for new apprentice electricians. The inclement weather was a huge challenge because he worked outside. His experience of several layoffs kept us barely supporting our large family, and keeping a decent roof over our head.

For three and a half years, Dave worked in Augusta, Georgia, at the Savannah River Plant. Later, he was transferred to another electrical job in Washington, DC, for three years. The children and I missed him terribly. When he'd surprise us and come home, we made it a holiday. When he left, the sad cloud returned. We dreamed when we could be together again.

I busily cared for our children with a driven vision. Whatever depression I experienced took a backseat. It was when I was alone that I felt the pains of my past—especially with my husband away. However, God was faithful. He kept me focused as a committed wife and mother, keeping our family together.

During this time, I became a Bible worker, sharing the Gospel of Christ with families in the community and assisting needy families. God truly was providing for us, and we wanted to pass the blessings along. Most importantly, we identified with their needs.

The children were part of this ministry, as the people looked forward to the visits, and the Lord laid a strong foundation. It gave me great security even though I knew other temptations and distractions could hurt them. I became a very strict parent while balancing PTA meetings, Bible work, and part-time classes at the university, helping our teenage sons mature without a full-time father, and protecting them from the distractions of the streets and drugs.

My other fear was not seeing Mama since I couldn't drive long distance.

One summer, Dave came home and bought us a Buick station wagon. It was a fine car. He couldn't drive us to Mississippi, so I learned by God's grace.

At first, I was scared, then calm when I realized how relaxed I was along the road. God always has a plan for his children. I should have known that by now. My past had left dreadful scars, and it didn't take much to worry.

Through my home girl, I was able to trail her and her family to Meridian, Mississippi, on one of our trips. There they directed me to Jackson. In faith, I kept driving, and soon we arrived at Mama's, safe and sound.

I credit a lot of my driving ability to my father. Whenever we rode with Daddy, I watched the way he handled the vehicle, his courtesy on the road, always stopping to let someone pass and nodding his head to salute or say hello. I pattern it still today. He took pride in his cars and required the same from us. As I learned to drive, I pictured my father right beside me, reminding me where to turn and how to back up. Thank you, Daddy! Thanks for your tough love.

For the next six and a half years, the Lord watched over the children and me as we traveled to Augusta, GA, Washington, DC, and Jackson and Bolton, Mississippi. We never had an accident. Praise the Lord!

It was during those years my heart found some peace and contentment along the road. The drive was very therapeutic, even with the children. We always had our preroad talks, about how we needed to focus on the trip. As I listened to my Christian tapes, they played road games and Bible trivia.

Upon arrival, Mama sent me to bed and cared for the children. The food was always ready. After noticing the growth and maturity of the children as grandparents do, she gave them chores, typical of my rearing on the farm.

Terrance, DJ, Kristie, and Kenny learned much from Mama about country life. We took baths in tin tubs, and our restroom was the outhouse. The children complained but were taught to respect and be thankful for what Granny was providing. They fed the chickens and slopped the hogs, as they say in the South. They helped with the laundry by hanging out and taking in the clothes off the line. They also picked vegetables from the large garden and waited as Mama prepared a feast fit for a king.

When it was time to say goodbye, she loaded the station wagon with food, clothes, quilts, and anything she could so we wouldn't have to buy it. Any available space in the car was used to store needed items to help our large struggling family survive.

When I arrived I arrived in Mississippi, my peace was short-lived. For years, I suffered with a nervous stomach, weight loss, anemia, and depression. I still carried the guilt as a traitor to Hunter. I knew one day there must be closure about our past.

On one particular visit, I heard rumors he had married a beautiful, Spanish American girl. I thought that must be his consolation for my betrayal. I knew that it wasn't true, but still, with whom could I share this burden? Then my mind returned to the day he cancelled our wedding. I buried the pain in the back of my mind and covered it with more depression…

The children and I enjoyed our visits to Augusta and DC. We visited sites such as the Jefferson and Washington monuments and saw nearby scenes of the capitol. We also tried new cuisine from the Georgetown area and attended church service on several occasions. It saddened our hearts when it was time to leave Dave and return to Knoxville.

A part of me stayed numbed all those years because I knew I had to survive for my children. So I embraced each challenge and found strength in Christ to press on.

I tried often to convince Dave to move us with him, but he didn't want the children's education interrupted every time the Union transferred him; also, he wasn't sure how long he would be in one place.

After our visit, we'd trail him part of the way to the interstate. Then he'd take an exit, and we'd continue home. Oh, my poor children cried their hearts out. I cried also inside but kept a steady eye on the road for all our sakes.

After driving for a while, the Lord settled and comforted my mind that He was with us, that one day we would be together again as a family. Dave would be home to stay. Often, I envisioned a special angel watching over us, especially when we drove through the mountains.

Because of my love for nature, I talked quietly to the trees and admired the stature of the mountains; the greenery of spring was a new awakening that God was with us through the unpredictable future.

The many colors of the fall leaves reminded me to reflect on the distance God had brought us, and trust Him to lead. However, fall meant a sad time, even now, and it is my favorite season of the year. In a sense, it reminded me that it's time for a change, a new vision, and to stay focused. I pray for courage during this fall of 2019, as I complete the final editing stages of my book.

While driving, I was always mindful to stay awake or rest if I got tired, because our four treasures depended on me. We sang and guessed the miles before the next exit. Then I gave treats to the winners.

Before we realized it, we had pulled into the driveway and thanked God for traveling mercies once again. Praise You, Lord. We often traveled during the night because sometimes we got a late start. My vision was excellent as I drove through the mountains. I basked in God's awesome handiwork and received a peace and contentment that was unexplainable. The tall trees and beautiful colors seemed to sympathize with my pain and encouraged me that one day I, too, would walk tall and leave the misery behind.

While Dave was working in Augusta, he suffered a ruptured hernia, resulting in major surgery.

It was the week before Christmas when his friend and coworker told us the hard news. Somehow, through the snow and taking the Atlanta route, I had to bring him home. It wouldn't be easy. It also meant making arrangements for the children. I couldn't travel through the North Carolina Mountains in the snow with them, not knowing where I was going.

My home girl offered to keep Kristie and Kenny so I could take T and DJ with me. They were leaving for Mississippi in a week. Also that if we didn't return in time, they would take Kristie and Kenny with them. I felt stuck between a boulder and a mountain.

The thought of my two small children being far from me was unbearable. But I had no one else to help. So I prayed and asked God to work it out. I knew they were in good hands because she and I had helped each other before.

It was a snowy winter. The only other route was going through Atlanta. The traffic would be terrible. But the boys and I had to go.

Later, we received word that Dave had survived the surgery and would be released in a week. I had to be there when he was discharged.

After getting Kristie and Kenny settled with the Davises, Terrance, DJ, and I started for Augusta, via Atlanta.

We arrived in Atlanta at night and got stuck in several lanes of traffic and couldn't find our exit for Augusta. DJ cried, "Mama, we are lost. We ain't ever gonna see Daddy." I said, "God is with us." I began to panic but couldn't let the boys know. I wanted to be brave, but the tears ran down my face as I prayed silently, hoping my sons wouldn't notice.

A stranger, perhaps our angel, rolled down his window and asked, "Where you trying to go lady?" I nervously responded as he showed me the exit to Augusta.

We arrived around midnight and met our friend James, who took us to the hospital. The boys and I were happy to see Dave, and he smiled in return.

After we checked him out of the hospital, we spent the next two days in our friend's home, permitting Dave to rest. However, we were anxious to get home before the Davis family left. By the end of the third day, we had miraculously arrived home to get our children. I will always be grateful for the Davis' kindness.

We picked up Kristie and Kenny and held them close. Our family was together for Christmas.

We spent two glorious months together as Dave healed from surgery. After the doctor released him, there was a new transfer from the union. He was going to DC in a few months. Our hearts sank.

However, I thanked God he was better and back on his feet. He was a terrible patient, couldn't keep him still. But we enjoyed having him home.

During those seven and a half years, our children adjusted well traveling great distances. After prayer, we'd leave early in the morning and arrive late in the evening.

We always stopped at the Alabama Welcome Center, the Trussville exit, and the Mississippi welcome center to gas up and refresh ourselves.

When we went to the restrooms, we stayed together, per Mama's instructions. My responsibilities were so great that, inside, I was afraid either the car would break down and we would be at the mercy of strangers, or I'd go to sleep at the wheel. So I pressed on, fearful but courageous, and Mama and the Holy Spirit were my coaches.

On a return trip from Mississippi, I had to confirm some rules with my children. They were restless, and I was tired. Mama always reminded them to obey, especially on the road.

On this particular trip, we were about seventy-five miles from Knoxville. DJ was playing with paper airplanes. Suddenly, one of them flew to the front of the car. It surprised me, and I almost lost control. I told him to stop and wait until we get home. "Yes, ma'am," he said quickly.

However, he continued. Suddenly, all of the children were having a field day, playing with airplanes, and no one listened to me. I couldn't focus on the road.

I pulled the car off the interstate and parked under an overpass. I didn't say a word as I got out the car. I turned and observed four sets of eyes watching me. I walked along the road and broke off two switches. I took each one out of the car and took care of business.

The cars passed by were looking, but I paid little attention. That day, our children learned a very valuable lesson: to obey Mama at all times, especially on the dangerous road.

After the obedience lesson, the children slept all the way home, and I was able to drive in peace. That day, the scripture "Chastise your children that you may have peace" was fulfilled in the Shingles family along I-75 North to Knoxville.

In the fall of 1989, I tried to go back to school. I wanted badly to get my degree. My failed college vision haunted me every time I received a graduation invitation. So I worked part-time teaching at a preschool day care and going to college part-time.

The stress of being Mom and Dad to four children was overwhelming. I rushed here and there, attending school events and balancing work, school, and home demands. I was falling apart inside but carried a tough facade on the outside.

Little did I realize that a small volcano was about to erupt and change our family's future.

One evening, I was rushing and ended up in a serious car accident with neck injuries. I foolishly collided with a semitractor trailer at the mall. I inadvertently passed in the wrong lane. The truck made a wide turn and lifted my station wagon off the ground. Kristie and Kenny were with me. The impact jolted my neck and head, and flared up some damaged muscles from a prior injury. Praise the Lord, the children wasn't injured in any way.

I got out of my car and told the driver he was at fault. Another passerby agreed with me. So that confirmed my belief. At the time, I couldn't see that I was at fault. I was in a state of denial and shock. We were immediately taken to the hospital and checked. The doctor confirmed that the children were fine, but I had severe neck and shoulder injuries.

Due to my disability, I was terminated from my job. Another shock! For the next several weeks, I underwent physical therapy. My emotions were here and there. I was stressed and depressed and felt so alone. Dave was working in DC, and I had so many decisions to make. He called daily to check in, but I needed him home.

I praised and thank God for the devotion of one of my church moms. Sis. Dawson stayed by my side the whole time. She took me to physical therapy every week and never complained. She is gone now, but I will never forget her kindness and patience.

I reported the accident to our insurance company, still believing the truck driver was at fault. The station wagon was drivable, but had sustained damage and needed repairs.

Dave was a good provider. In addition to sending money home to support us, he still had to pay for expensive lodging. We stayed borderline trying to pay our bills. Also, we didn't have extra money to repair the car, because we were still paying a car note.

The credit union investigated and learned that I was at fault. I was shocked again, even devastated, because we were expecting a settlement from my injuries. All we received were bills that our insurance didn't pay. But at least I knew the truth.

I felt terrible for Dave, myself, and the children.

The credit union repossessed and repaired my precious little station wagon that carried the children and me all those years. Now, it was gone.

When I was alone, I cried uncontrollably because we had no transportation. Our second car had stopped running, so Dave was carpooling between Knoxville and DC with one of his buddies from a nearby county. We didn't know what to do but to keep on praying.

Dave felt bad, leaving so much on me. However, I blamed myself.

One wintry, snowy night, after putting the children to bed, I slowly walked out on the porch, feeling overwhelmed.

Suddenly, I saw this big man coming toward the house. I became frightened and started back inside. Then I recognized him. It was my husband. I had not seen him in months. He had grown a large beard. I was still wearing a neck support.

He came upon the porch and picked me up and held me close and said, "I am home. I have given up the road and come home to take care of you and the children. I will find whatever work to support us. But for now, my place is here." I was thrilled to have him home. But how would we support our family?

However, he never went back on the road. The children were so glad to have their father home; so was I.

Our other dilemma was trying to feed our children. Neither one of us had a job. But God didn't forget us. He provided through any public assistance we were eligible for. We accepted it! No time for foolish pride! The children had to be provided for.

During this time, all my rearing and upbringing were invaluable. I stretched a dollar and prepared a meal out of nothing, as I continued to heal. Thanks to Mama and Daddy's training and God's mercy. I so wanted to work, but the doctor hadn't released me.

The following spring, the doctor said I could work part-time. Dave tried to find work, but no one was hiring electricians, especially someone still relatively new to the trade, and the inclement weather was very challenging.

God still worked behind every disappointment. One of our church members, Sis. Kelsey, at the State Employment Office sympathized with our dilemma and offered to help. She assured us that God would open doors, just don't stop praying.

She sent us on various interviews with free bus passes.

I was hired as a newspaper telemarketer. For the first few weeks, I did well. Every week, I'd notice the supervisor laying pink slips on the desk of my coworkers. I said, "Surely that lady won't pink slip me with what I'm going through."

However, the following week, my sales were drastically low. The supervisor walked by my desk, looked sadly in my eyes, and said, "I'm sorry," and laid a pink slip on my desk.

I walked to the bus stop and agonized with God over our situation. I boarded the bus and cried as I looked out the window. A nice lady tried to console me, but it was little help. I thanked her but could only focus on the loss of my job.

The following week, we returned to the Employment Office. Dave still hadn't found any work.

One day, Sis. Kelsey sent us on interviews with Knox County Schools District in Knoxville. Praise God, we were hired the same day!

In the spring of 1990, I was hired as a part-time front desk receptionist/lunchroom monitor at Green Elementary School. Dave was hired as a custodian at South Young High School. I worked three months until school closed for the summer. The principal was very pleased with my work, and I loved my job. When it was time to get off at twelve noon, I didn't want to leave. I found lots of excuses to stay later. However, I had to abide by the doctor's statement.

Early that summer, the doctor released me to work full-time. I received a call from Green Elementary School for an interview.

I was hired as secretary-bookkeeper in August of 1990, beginning a twenty-four-year journey serving the Green School family. I claimed the Holy Spirit's guidance daily as I worked and prayed diligently with some of the greatest administrators, faculty and staff, parents and students, and community partners I have ever known. For twenty-four years, I witnessed God connecting pieces to the puzzle in my family and the many families of Green Magnet Math and Science Academy.

All the challenges that Dave, the children, and I endured drew us closer to God and closely knitted our family. We learned to depend solely on Him for everything.

Through each challenge, we taught our children to always *"Trust in the Lord with all thine heart; and lean not unto thine own understanding. In all thy ways acknowledge Him and He shall direct thy paths" (Prov. 3:5–6).*

*"The Lord will
perfect that which concerneth me: thy mercy,
O Lord, endureth for ever: forsake not the works of thine hands."*

—*Ps. 138:8*

Chapter 11

THE FINAL PARTING

During the fall of 2001, Hunter and I mysteriously met again after thirty years.

I was experiencing ill health, stress of keeping two children in college, and staying focused on my job. I longed to travel, listen to my therapy music, and commune with God.

Deep in my heart, I knew the closure between Hunter and I had to come, someday. I didn't realize it would be so soon.

I called my sister Susan and told her I was coming for a visit.

She had moved to a new place and started a new season of her life. This was a great opportunity to see how she and her daughter were doing. I also needed some old-fashioned sister talk.

Then she said Hunter was home visiting his brother and asked for my telephone number. I hesitated and said okay.

Hunter called, and it was painful to hear his voice after so long. It reminded me that my heart hadn't completely healed. He asked if I was coming home anytime soon. That it had been thirty years since we had seen each other and it was okay for old classmates to see each other. I said I wasn't sure. But in my heart, I couldn't handle seeing him. We asked about each other's family and then hung up.

In addition to my present stress, I needed closure so I could move on emotionally and spiritually. I desired happiness with my family without the guilt and pain.

I told Dave I was thinking about going to Mississippi to visit my sister. I hadn't been back since Mama's funeral, and I wanted to visit her grave.

He knew I hadn't healed from the loss of our mother in 2000.

As I reflect, I remember Mama had suddenly become ill. It startled all of us. She was rarely sick, even with a cold. This was a woman who washed her family's clothes on the washboard and hung them outside in thirty-two-degree weather and trusted God to dry them. Miraculously, the Lord sent some sunshine and dried them. Otherwise, we took them off the line frozen, and used the fireplace to dry.

Before Mama became ill, Kenny and I paid her a special visit. He had graduated from high school, the spring of 1999. Mama wanted to see and spend time with the graduate. They were alike in many ways, such as ironing, folding clothes and making a bed.

When we arrived at her home, she didn't have her usual energy. I asked if she was ok, and she said, "yes." However, we talked long hours as usual, as she prepared our favorite meals. I didn't know the next time I'd see her, she would be in the hospital.

The morning Kenny and I prepared for home, a part of me didn't want to leave. After giving her a big hug, I felt the need to leave the car and hug her again, holding on to her, and looking into her eyes. That would be the last time I'd feel her arms around me in her home.

Kenny and I drove in silence as I looked back at Mama standing in the door. We called when we arrived in Knoxville, letting her know we had arrived safely.

That fall, September of 1999, I received an urgent call that my brother had found her collapsed on the floor. She was taken to the hospital and admitted for congestive heart failure and diabetes. I came home on several occasions to help care for her in the hospital, not believing that she was actually there.

Mama was a whole different person." She became depressed, saying she would never return home." We tried to persuade her otherwise. She kept her eyes closed and stopped speaking to us; only opened them if we said certain key words. "I'd say, "Mama, I'm here;

I love you". She'd look at me and turn her head away. I believed she was worried about something, but didn't know how to tell us.

Over a period of several months from September of 1999 to April of 2000, we took turns caring for our mother until she finally closed her eyes, bidding farewell to her eleven babies. We prayed she would pull through despite the doctor's diagnosis.

When I received the call that Mama was gone, I became numb. I couldn't believe or accept it. I couldn't cry either.

In our mind, our mother was invincible. She wasn't supposed to die. Suddenly, everything was different because Mama was gone. I felt loneliness beyond comprehension. The sky was different; and the trees and the leaves seemed to stand still. Everything was so quiet. As I walked around my backyard, I screamed her name and called, "Mama, Mama, where are you?"

She had always been there for us, her church, community, and the strangers she met.

If Mama knew you were in need and she could help, then help was on the way. She didn't stand by idly and watch people suffer. She was the scripture in shoes: "As you have done it unto the least of these my brethren, you have done it unto me."

We laid our mother to rest in April of 2000, bidding farewell to a matriarch of the ages, an icon of a mother and friend. The community would never be the same. Neither would we.

Whenever I drove home, I felt her presence in the trees and nature. I could hear her speaking to me through the old hymns we sang in the old Baptist church.

When we traveled to Mississippi, I couldn't wait to see her. Every town and exit reminded us how close we were to the matriarch of matriarchs.

By the time we stopped at the Mississippi welcome center, she could breathe some, knowing we were a little over two hours away, To go back now, with her gone, added double stress and grief.

As I was thinking about going home, Dave asked, "If Hunter is home, are you going to see him? " I said, 'I don't know." I asked, "if I do, are you okay with that? He said "yes." From the past with

Hunter and Sean, Dave didn't doubt my love and devotion to he and the children; and I didn't want him to.

When our children became teenagers, I felt impressed to share my past with them. I didn't want them to repeat the mistakes I had or to see me as some perfect person. I wanted them to share and communicate with me about anything on their hearts. It was my hope the experiences I went through, would serve as a testimony of what God can do, despite life setbacks.

Traditionally, when I'm driving out of town, I'd leave before sunrise to avoid the night driving—especially when alone. However, I got a late start.

I arrived in Jackson around midnight. I didn't know exactly where Susan's new place was. She had given me directions, but I couldn't find it. It was so dark! So I pulled over to a service station and called. Her line was busy. I tried over and over again. Still busy!

Then I called one of my brothers, and he didn't answer. I called another brother and no answer. I continued to call Susan repeatedly and kept getting a busy signal. I said, "Surely she has call waiting and can see that I am calling," but still no response.

Then I panicked! I said to myself, "Here I am almost home and lost." Fact of the matter is, I never learned to drive in Jackson before I moved to Knoxville. I just drove in the country.

Suddenly, I felt alone and started to cry. Then I remembered someone who wasn't far away who perhaps could help. I said to myself, "No, no way!" And that little voice said, "But Hunter is home, and you may have his number in your phone... Call him! I can't call. This will be too embarrassing and humiliating."

However fear overcame my pride, and I called. His older brother answered, and I shared my dilemma. I heard him say, "Hunter, Georgia Ann is on the phone." He came to the phone and said, "Peach, tell me where you are, and we'll come and get you." I said, "But I..." "No," he said, "we'll come get you."

I drove to Wal-Mart parking lot, and within twenty minutes, a car pulled up. This tall sky figure ran over to my car. "Peach, Peach, Ms. America, good to see you! Just follow us to the house, and we'll try to reach your sister."

I had such mixed feelings about going with them, but it was late, and I was tired and needed help.

At last, we arrived at his brother's home. I was invited to rest and make myself comfortable.

Hunter sat across from me and smiled. "Peach, Ms. America." I had my guard up. I couldn't relax with him. I didn't want to cast a shadow on my commitment to my husband and family with this man, not even in a conversation. So I acted nonchalant.

Then he asked for my sister's number. He called, and this time she answered. As his usual humorous self, he asked, "How come y'all won't answer the phone? Got Peach driving all over Jackson trying to find you. Y'all ought to be ashamed of yourself." Then he began laughing as Susan fussed at him on the other end. Later, she thought it was funny that I had mysteriously ended up there.

She came right over, and they teased each other like years ago, and then we went to her home. I was teased all night about how Hunter and I strangely met again.

The next day, Hunter invited me to visit his father in a rehabilitation home. I hesitated and said okay. His father looked well and remembered me. Then we went to our old high school.

We stood where we had boarded and departed bus #90 on many occasions. Then we hugged, standing near the bus area, knowing it would be the last time we'd see each other at our old alma mater. It wasn't a romantic hug. It was about two pitiful brokenhearted people, that somehow survived thirty years of life's hard challenges, with wounds and scars, and came together again to say goodbye.

Later, we visited my older brother in Edwards, Mississippi, but he wasn't home.

When we started back to Clinton, I decided it was time to tell him what had been on my heart for thirty-one years. I blurted out, "No longer will I carry the guilt of betrayal for our past. Many people didn't even know we had called off our relationship before I met Sean and became pregnant. You allowed them to think I betrayed you when we weren't even together. Have you any idea what it's been like, to know that every time I came home, I carried the guilt that my family and community saw me as a betrayer of someone's trust?"

I was so angry with him. I also said, "Most of all, it was you who called off our wedding. Do you know what that did to my mind? I almost lost it."

He looked so sad and said, "Peach, I know, and I'm sorry. At the time, so many people were telling me to do this and that. I wasn't sure what I was doing most of the time."

It was then I felt sorry for him. I began to wonder if this man had suffered as much brokenness as I had or even more.

When he asked about my family, I showed him a picture of my four young adult children. He looked and said, "You have a fine family." I thank him and then pointed out Terrance, who was no longer a little baby but a tall fine young man.

He turned and dropped his head.

Before we departed, I told him we must be committed to our families and hang in there. I also reminded him to accept Jesus as his Savior if he hadn't. He thanked me for the advice, and said, "You were always known for being so spiritual."

The following day, I was to return to Tennessee. Hunter called later that evening, and asked if we could have an early breakfast, before I got on the road. It seemed harmless, so I said yes.

When I called to confirm our breakfast appointment the following morning, he sounded in turmoil. Finally, we decided to leave everything as it were. We wished each other well and said goodbye.

When I got on the road, tears flooded my face. I cried, "Oh, Lord, why is so much pain still there? Help me, Lord, and help him. I can't drive five hundred miles in this condition."

Then the Lord reminded me in a song of the blessings He had given and that I must continue to trust him. Though I didn't understand, He would strengthen me to endure and that Hunter was only permitted in my life, through my choices; to teach a valuable, spiritual lesson; that Jesus must always be first.

In my heart, God revealed my beautiful family, waiting and depending on me to return and faithfully know that my resilient faith in Christ will sustain me. Trusting God, I arrived home safely and at peace.

Our fortieth-year class reunion was refreshing but bittersweet. I saw classmates I hadn't seen in forty years. Some had changed much, and time had barely touched some. Many said I looked great. As we renewed our acquaintances, I couldn't help but wonder what was their perception of me. Finally, I put it out of my mind and enjoyed the reunion.

I was a little disappointed that Hunter wasn't there but in a way relieved, because I still wondered what was on everyone's mind. My sister Susan accompanied me and was a strong support. She knew the reunion would reflect past hurts. She never left my side.

The next day at the reunion picnic, Hunter's best friend said he was on his phone and wanted to speak with me. We spoke briefly and reminded each other there would always be a special place in our hearts that only the Lord understood, and we would keep our respective families in prayer. Then we said goodbye again, not knowing it was truly the final parting.

It was around the end of December of 2011 when my brother Tim called and said, Hunter had a massive heart attack and died suddenly. I didn't know what to say. I wanted to be angry with him for giving me such tragic news. I was in shock for weeks. I tried to cry but couldn't, just relived our past and asked, "Why Hunter?"

Susan was a big comfort, as we relived old memories and understood that we must move on. I was so thankful God allowed us some closure. I prayed God's comfort for his family as well as myself, and to believe He was with us.

Hunter's passing, forced me to understand something very significant.

I had made this man invincible, an icon in my heart. Only Christ deserves that glory. He alone gave His life for us. I had little by little permitted this feeble human being to take Christ rightful place in my heart.

To those who are still reading my book, I hope you can finally see as God has opened my eyes that only "He can grant a peace to those whose mind is stayed on Him and trust in thee" (Isa. 26:3).

"Call unto me, and I will answer thee and show thee great and mighty things, which thou knowest not."

—*Jer. 33:3*

Chapter 12

THE VISION AND TRUTH

I retained the vision—to one day—finish college. When I left in 1972, it was no longer a reality. Years later, I prayed to fulfill it for my parents and my family who believed in me. It was a constant void that I couldn't shake.

After Dave and I married, it was obvious with a growing family—I would never accomplish that dream.

During our children's post high school and college prep years, I became aware of something. We had prepared the children for college and trusted God to bring it to fruition. Still my vision was hanging in the balance. I was asking them to fulfill their vision but hadn't set the example. To preserve it, we made an agreement. "If they complete their education, no matter how hard it is, one day I would complete mine."

It became evident during our children's college prep years, that I was asking them to fulfill a vision that I hadn't accomplished. To preserve our vision, we agreed to complete our education, regardless how challenging.

That gave me the motivation to get started with God's leading.

Deciding to go back to school was a big step. I worked during the day and attended classes at night. The thought that I'd be going to school with my children's generation was frightening, despite the few that attended from my generation.

Returning to college was a huge adjustment. The students' language was difficult to understand, especially with my hearing issues. They were super computer whizzes. I constantly asked for help and to speak slowly or repeat a statement." *The thought of taking courses such as college algebra, business in a global society, etc., clouded my thinking.*

As I trusted God about this mountain, I found that staying in His Word provided the balance I needed. God must be glorified through every challenge. I must believe His Word and act on it. For example, James 1:5 was a reminder that "If any man lacks wisdom, let him ask of God that giveth freely and upbraideth not."

As I struggled in class, one of my professors noticed how well I performed in composition writing. Soon the learning teams were contended to have me as a member. My self esteem as a class member elevated.

Some of my classmates saw me as a mother figure. Those of my generation became my buddies, and we chatted constantly about our challenge to keep up. We cried each night as we left class knowing we would fail. But we always came back the next night, determined to see it through.

I gained the respect of many of my fellow students. I was able to share some of my past experiences to help them get a different perspective on life and spiritual values.

My professors were kind, patient and always available for tutoring. I learned much and will always cherish my two and a half years at the college.

On December 19, 2009, by God's grace, we struggled through the ice and snow with my family to Greeneville, Tennessee. It was there, at age fifty-seven, that God blessed me to graduate from Tusculum College receiving a Bachelor's of Science degree in organizational management. It fulfilled a vision to my children, parents, and many I had nurtured and mentored along the way that nothing is too hard for God. This accomplishment held a special meaning for me and our son DJ, who graduated from this same college several years earlier.

After graduation, we drove back to Knoxville and celebrated my fulfilled vision. However, it was a bittersweet celebration because all of my children were not there.

Kristie and Terrance were stranded by a severe snowstorm that hit the Virginia and DC areas. Terrance flight was cancelled, and Kristie and her friend were stranded in the snow in Virginia. Still, we praised God for their safety.

When Dave and I married, T and I were faithfully attending a small Baptist church in Knoxville. I felt nurtured and content with the members, especially the pastor's wife who was kind to our children. When they discovered I was a Christian and knew some Bible, I was invited to teach the Sunday school class.

Dave joined later and was baptized when DJ was a baby. Daily, we studied God's Word diligently and tried to rear our children with Christian values.

Somehow, I felt something missing from my spiritual life. There was a lack of fulfillment in my prayers and studying God's Word. I continued to study and prayed for guidance.

It was during the summer of 1981 that we met and befriended a dear distinguished man. His name was Elder Richard Myers.

I was expecting Kenny, our fourth child, and miserable from the heat. Dave and I were sitting on the front porch when he stopped by. He was casually but neatly dressed and immediately reminded me of my father.

As a literature evangelist, he was canvassing and selling books in the community. He spoke eloquently and shared some unusual information pertaining to the Bible in question and answer format.

My immediate expression revealed that I wasn't interested, though it piqued my curiosity. I knew the words were true because I had read them in the Bible.

He read scriptures about God's Ten Commandments, that we are to love Him and obey His statutes. Then he read something about the Sabbath Day that I hadn't heard before, that God hadn't changed His Holy Sabbath Day. Misguided men had changed it hundreds of years ago for the sake of convenience and compromise, and there is no biblical basis for keeping Sunday. He read excerpts from different denominations that professed Saturday as the seventh-day Sabbath, but did not observe it.

One particular denomination boasted about the change from Saturday to Sunday. This interested me as I turned to look at this gentleman reading with boldness and confidence. I felt compelled to agree with him. Still I made no effort to inquire further or that I was interested in the book.

After he finished reading, Dave said, "We'll purchase the book *Bible Readings for the Home*." Thank the Lord for impressing his heart.

By purchasing this book, the door was opened to a great friendship and much enlightenment. He offered to study the Bible with us, but we refused and thanked him.

However something kept bothering me about this strange man. Here he was in the hot, humid weather sharing God's Word without apology. The words held some meaning, but I couldn't make the connection.

Elder Myers continued to canvass our neighborhood and stopped by for water and small talk. The children and I chatted through the screen door, still cautious about his intentions.

Again he offered Bible studies, but I said we were still praying about it. One day as he was leaving, I felt impressed to ask when we could begin Bible studies. Filled with joy, he happily said we could begin immediately.

For the next several months, Elder Myers and our family studied the Bible on topics as God's Holy Sabbath, what happens to man when he dies, Bible prophecies, our body as God's temple, and many other subjects from God's Word. We didn't know there were so many scriptures on a particular topic.

As we continued studying, we discovered a conflict with the teachings of our church, so we decided to share them with our Sunday school class. As their teacher, I thought they wanted to know also.

One Sunday morning after Sunday school class, the pastor asked about the peculiar class discussion.

I told him we were taking Bible studies and had learned some Bible truths we wanted to share with the class.

He immediately cautioned me not to share such teachings, because the church didn't believe or teach such things. I tried to explain, but he brushed my comments aside. However, we continued to study the Bible and pray.

We shared our concerns with Elder Myers and asked for guidance. He informed us that he was a member of a Bible-teaching church and we should continue to pray, study, and allow God to guide us. Then he invited us to visit his church family.

We didn't want to leave our little church family we had grown to love, especially the pastor's wife. Somehow, we felt trapped between obeying God and man. In our hearts, we knew that we must obey God.

However, we kept going to our church until the conflict became overwhelming. We couldn't continue violating our conscience, knowing what we had learned. However, we weren't ready to join a new church either.

One particular Sunday, Dave decided to go back to our church, but I couldn't go with him. After trying to persuade me differently, he went alone and informed the church of our pending decision. I felt pretty cowardly letting him go alone, but I couldn't continue to teach false doctrine.

While home with the children, I watched the clock hour by hour wondering if he had spoken to the congregation.

Around 1:30 p.m., he came home looking disappointed but somewhat relieved. He had informed them we had considered joining the Seventh Day Adventist Church.

They aggressively told him, "We were confused and were joining a cult and that any day is acceptable to God." Suddenly, he asked if we were doing the right thing. I suggested we pray for God's guidance. We took our Bible and reviewed all we had studied. Again, God's Word confirmed what we'd already learned, that God want us to love and obey Him, despite what man says.

It was the summer of 1982 when the building of the new Adventist church was completed. Service was held in another church while the new church was erected. Elder Myers helped when he was not selling books. Dave and I decided to attend his church.

We attended on several occasions learning greater Bible knowledge. The members and the pastor and his wife were very kind and happy to see us.

Elder Myers faithfully picked us up for church since we didn't have a car. He was a missionary at heart, helping with the children. No matter how cold it was, we were eager to go when he arrived, wrapping the children up warmly, especially in the freezing weather. Even though it was cold outside, when we entered the Adventist church, it was a warm, caring atmosphere. We sensed a confirmation that this was where God wanted us to be.

The last day he visited us, it was bittersweet news. He was moving to Florida join his family. We were heartbroken. For many months, he had taught us the Word, but we hadn't joined the new church. He respected our decision, knowing his responsibility was to present the Bible truth. It was our decision to accept it. We had left our church but hadn't joined another. Dave and I wanted to be sure the messages we learned was a solid foundation to teach our children.

We felt trapped in the midst of uncertainty. He had been our primary contact with the new truths and the new church, and we had grown very fond of him. We were entering a new world. Still, we trusted that God would lead us, though we felt like lost sheep. We sought God in prayer and continued to visit the new church.

"The Lord's our Rock, in Him we hide,
A shelter in the time of storm;
Secure whatever ill betide
A shelter in the time of storm."

—*SDA Hymnal, #528*

Chapter 13

THE MIRACULOUS SHELTER

One day, the Adventist pastor and his wife visited our home. Her compliment of our home and the children's conduct helped me relax.

She knew we were struggling to provide for our children. She'd say, "Now, Georgia, these children will not remain this age and size forever. Don't worry about what you can't give them. Continue to teach them God's Word and model the best, and God will supply the rest. Then she recited a text, "For I will contend with him that contendeth with thee, and I will save thy children" (Isa. 49:25). Praise God for that promise.

I continued to cry to God for a better place. I also remembered Mama's counsel to always be thankful for what you have. It was a monthly hardship trying to pay our bills.

We were still attending the Adventist church. I learned to study God's Word in great depth, strengthening my relationship with the Lord and my prayer life.

Daily, I looked out my kitchen window praying, and trying not to worry.

One day, I noticed a vacant house across the street. I didn't see anyone coming or going and wondered if anyone lived there. Strangely, the house disturbed me as I studied it daily.

One Sabbath, the Adventist church asked for pledges for the church building fund. By this time, we were almost convinced that we belonged here, though we hadn't joined. Dave and I looked at each other and agreed that our rent money should be given to help. It was all we had. We didn't worry how we were going to make it. We simply trusted God and gave with a cheerful heart, thanking Him that we had something to share. He had shared graciously with us through His manservant. Then we made a pledge to give again and believed God would provide.

Dave was continually laid off work. We applied regularly to an agency that assisted with utility bills.

The staff was helpful in completing the paperwork, treating us with respect, not as undeserving. Our children were instructed to obey and remain seated until we finished. We didn't know we were being observed.

One day, the agency called me at work, stating that trustees were looking for a reliable family, to maintain and clean their church and grounds, in exchange for rent-free parsonage/residence. They would only be responsible for the utilities.

The agency had referred our family to them. If we were interested, we should submit three character references to the trustees within two weeks. I immediately said, "Yes, ma'am, we are very interested. I thanked her over and over again. Then I let out a big "Thank You, Jesus," right there in the school office.

I immediately asked for references from my supervisors. Dave said he would speak with his boss as well.

We were nervous as we arrived to the appointment. The trustees were retired, older gentlemen with serious faces and lots of questions.

We answered their questions the best we could and trusted God. After the interview, we were told that two other families would be interviewed. My hopes were dashed, because I thought we were the only family applying. They promised to contact us in two weeks regarding their decision.

Then they asked if we wanted to see the house. We immediately said yes.

When we were given the address, I was shocked that it was the house I had noticed from my window.

I kept saying, "Lord, is it possible?" We will finally have a better place to live and raise our children. Besides a thorough cleaning and scrubbing, it needed painting inside and outside. The floors were coated with hard wax over dirt, and the walls were painted black. Still, we looked at each other and said, "We can work with it."

The two weeks seemed like two years. Finally, we received the call we had been waiting for. We had been chosen to reside in the house. I screamed and praised God!

All my coworkers including the principal rejoiced with me even though they hadn't seen it… They just knew with our faith in God, it was something special.

It was agreed that we would do the inside painting and the property manager would do the rest.

The utilities was turned on, so the house would be warm for our children as we cleaned.

For two weeks, Dave and I scrubbed, cleaned, and painted until the house was ready for occupying.

Because electric work was so unstable, Dave left the trade to try Job Corps. It would mean a regular paycheck and flying to Utah for a week of training.

It was in the winter, and we had a few days to move before he left. We missed him terribly as we adjusted to our new home.

Every morning, I walked through the house praising and thanking God He had chosen us to be here. Praise His name!

We continued to attend the Adventist church, and one Saturday/Sabbath in the summer of 1982, we joined the College Hill Seventh Day Adventist Church through baptism. Oh, what a joyous day.

Knoxville was hosting the 1982 World's Fair. We wanted to go but didn't have any money. However, when we became Seventh Day Adventist Christians, we rejoiced and had our world's fair at home. We continued to study God's Word and raised our children in the church, praying they would follow the Lord's leading.

However, we missed Elder Myers. For all the nurturing, he wasn't there to see us baptized. It was a bittersweet time and would be many years before we see him again.

Dave worked at Job Corps for two years. The pay was fair, but he was constantly coming home bruised from breaking up fights.

One day, he received an offer from the union to go on the road as an apprentice-wireman. The children and I would miss him terribly, but at least he could support us. That meant the children and I would have to clean and maintain the church and yard during his absence.

It wasn't easy working a full-time job, caring for four growing children, a house, a large church, and a yard since we had no other family here. Because God had been so faithful, I knew He would supply the strength and wisdom to carry this responsibility, because He had orchestrated it from the beginning.

The children were young, but taught to work. The church had several classrooms, a large sanctuary, basement fellowship area and a large front and back yard.

Everyone was trained to clean their area with my assistance. DJ and Terrance were older and large enough to help with larger tasks. I was still suffering with ill health and always exhausted after we finished.

Sometimes, I'd hear T and DJ complain, "How come we have to clean this church? We want to play and have fun like the other children?"

One cold fall day, I came home not feeling well. I knew we had to clean the church and mow the yard, so I asked T and DJ to walk to the church and get started on their areas, and the smaller children and I would come later. The church was located behind our home, so they didn't have far to go.

As I was preparing our meal, I overheard some grumbling and talking outside. I looked out the window, and it was my boys complaining again. To hear them complain again was too much. I decided to teach them a lesson.

I called out the window and told them, "Hey, boys, don't worry about cleaning the church. The younger children and I will do it after I finish supper. In the meantime, since you are not cleaning the church, you have to remain outside since you don't have any place to stay." They said, "Mama, what do you mean?" I said, "Well, remember, we are living here under a contract which says we clean the church and yard. If we don't, we can't live here. So I'm sorry, you all can't come inside."

By this time, it was really getting cold. DJ started crying, and he and T started blaming each other for complaining. DJ said, "Mama, can we please come inside? It's getting cold out here." I said, "No, you can't, and it's going to get even colder. I hope you have on your jackets.

Then they started arguing again. "Man, it's your fault for complaining." By that time, DJ was crying loudly, "Mama, please, please let us in to warm up, and we will go and clean the church." T hadn't said very much. He was trying to be proud.

Suddenly, I heard from him, "Mama, please let us in to get warm. It ain't cool now. It is cold, and we will clean the church." I said, "No, this may happen again, so I think you all need to give this some thought. We won't be going through this again. That means I will have to tell your father to send some money to hire someone to help me and the younger children clean the church." "Mama, please don't do that," they said.

By that time, they were at the door, crying their eyes out, saying, "Mama, we are so sorry. We didn't mean it. We know you are tired. We will help you."

I wanted to cry, but I held back the tears. However, I was crying inside for my boys, but I had to teach and prepare them for a challenging future. They had to learn discipline and work and be thankful for what God had provided.

Finally, I let them in to get warm. After that, they ran up to the church. When they left, I went to my room, closed the door, and cried for the lesson I had to teach my boys. I said, "Lord, I know it seemed cruel. But I can't raise selfish, lazy children. I want them to be resourceful and work, serve You and others, and most of all, be thankful. It is hard raising our children alone, but I know you are with me. Please help me train these children to be good, earthly and heavenly citizens."

After cooking supper, we joined them and completed the church work. I didn't have to repeat that lesson again. But many more lessons were taught along the road, at home, in school, and in church. Most of all, we learned from each other. Thank You, Lord.

After we cared and maintained the church for several years, the pastor met me at the clothesline and said the church would close.

On the front of the newspaper was a large sad article about the death of a church in the community. I asked what would be our future with the house. She said a trustee would be in touch with us.

Later, we were assigned to clean and maintain a church across town. We had to drive several miles. It would be a hardship, but we had to keep our agreement. We cleaned this church for two years.

One day, I received another call at work. It was the Church Conference Committee thanking us for our service. They asked, "How would you like the house for a Christmas gift?" It would be ours for free. It needed a lot of repairs, and they were unable to do it. Without a thought, I said yes, praised God, and thanked them for their generosity.

When I informed my coworkers of the news, they remarked, "You must be a praying woman. What else are you praying for?"

We received our deed to the house and thanked the Lord for his mercies. However, by this time, the house had deteriorated in several areas, and we had no money for repairs. We did whatever we could to keep it in decent shape.

I prayed and asked the Lord for help—that if he gave us the house in this condition, He would restore it to His glory.

I continued to keep our home before the Lord. The ceiling was cracking, and the bathroom and kitchen floors were buckling. It became too bad for us to reside there, but we had no place to go. Still I called it "my little mansion."

One day, I left work early not feeling well. I drove through an area of town as if someone was directing me where to go. I stopped at an agency and went in. I asked the lady what services they provided. She explained the application process for home renovations from the city.

I looked at photos of homes like ours that had been renovated. It was miraculous. She volunteered to complete the application. She had the demeanor of a sweet angel. There was a presence there that was so peaceful. Later, I knew that the Lord was leading me that day.

When the application was completed, she put it in an envelope and asked me to mail it to the city with a ten-dollar-money order. I would receive a response in several weeks.

I continued to pray for our home, and as time passed, I actually forgot about the application. We continued to maintain the best we could and prayed help would come soon.

That summer, as the children and I were sitting in the family room playing Bible games, two large brown envelopes arrived in the mail. They were home rehabilitation letters, stating we had been approved for the complete renovation of our home. We were so happy. All of us screamed! I know the neighbors heard us. We couldn't believe it! The letters listed the amount that was approved for renovations. It was a three percent rehabilitation loan payable to the city over a twenty-year period. It would also provide a place for us to live while our home was being renovated—hopefully somewhere close in our neighborhood so our children wouldn't have to change schools.

The Lord had worked in mysterious ways, His wonders to perform. Our neighbor offered her rental home. Another miracle!

We put our major furniture items and appliances in storage and were free to use items in her home such as stove, washer and dryer, and kitchen appliances.

It was a grand blessing, because the house was next door to our home. We could check on it during the renovation.

The Lord blessed us to move back within a year.

For the next twenty years to the present, we have resided in our home, rearing our children in the Lord, and blessed to see our grandchildren, walk in the footprints of their parents, when they were children.

God blessed us to pay off the rehabilitation mortgage on March 2, 2015, thus making us sole owners/stewards and God the Sole Provider, free of a mortgage. Praise the Lord! We are a witness that God truly provides a miraculous shelter! Hallelujah!

"He healeth the broken in heart, and bindeth up their wounds."

—Psalms 147:3

Chapter 14

The Rose Blooms

In summary, as I bring this book to a close, I ask myself, "Georgia, what have you learned from these experiences?" I pondered and then remembered some quotes from one of Charles Swindoll's messages that sums it well.

He said, "During my seminary years, one of my mentors, Dr. Bruce Waltke said, "God rarely, if ever explains why. One thing is for sure, when that door closes, we do not think at that moment, this is going to lead me to something better."

He quotes the Scottish essayist, Thomas Carlyle, 19th century writer, essayist, historian, "when the oak tree is felled, the whole forest echoes with it; but a hundred acorns are planted silently by some unnoticed breeze. When the door slams in our face, we don't think that poetically. All we can hear is the falling of our oak and the thud as it hits the forest; destroying our dream, our hope, our anticipation. We don't think at that moment that there are some acorns being whisked away and blown to a place, that will grow and bear fruit for God's glory through an open door.

His 4 guidelines regarding an open/closed door helped me understand my journey of adversity and courage; that "God is in the heavens, He does whatever He pleases." Also…

1. Since God is Sovereign, He is in full control on both sides of any door.

2. Being in full control, God takes responsibility for the results.
3. The closing of a good opportunity occurs in order to lead us to an even better one.
4. Not until you walk through the open door and look back, you realize the necessity of the other door being closed."

So reader, a small breeze blew a special acorn (me) to Knoxville, Tennessee. I am also a rose that endured adversity to bring forth blooms, among the thorns. It is my prayer that you have grown through these pages. You have journey with me through much. You have smiled and laughed through my joys, and cried with me through my disappointments, tears and pain.

I hope to keep learning that:

My trust and joy must be found in God and Him alone, not people.

It is an unjust burden and responsibility to expect others to be the ultimate source of our joy, when they too are pressed with life challenges.

That when our hope is in God, despite the unexpected and unpredictable challenges that come; it may surprise us, but will not unsettle us. The Rock of Ages will hold us steady.

May God bless you and thanks for investing your time and resources in my book, my life, my family.

As always, I say, "Take care."
Ms. Georgia

"Do not watch the petals fall from the roses with sadness; know that, like life, things sometimes must fade, before they can bloom again."

—*Unknown*

About the Author

Georgia Shingles is a retired Secretary/Bookkeeper. She passionately serves her community and church as outreach minister, elder, and assist with the church Burundi ministry. Through her vegetarian/vegan cuisine business, she shares original and Southern dishes, promoting "selective eating with a vision." She serves on two community activist boards, which fosters positive, community awareness, service, and promotes health and wellness.

On June 2, 2001, her family was awarded first place in the "2001 Celebrating the Enduring Black Family Gold Pyramid Award" in Knoxville, Tennessee, by Delta Sigma Theta Sorority, Inc. Knoxville Alumnae Chapter.

On June 15, 2001, her family was awarded "Honoring Your Dedication to Faith, Family and Community Award," from the Church of Jesus Christ of Latter Day Saints, Knoxville Cumberland Stake in Knoxville, Tennessee.

On September 1, 2018, Georgia was presented the Distinguished Service Award by the Mechanicsville Community Association, for her generous commitment of time, support and inspiration in the neighborhood, at the MCA's 13th Annual Homecoming, Knoxville, Tennessee.

She resides in Knoxville, Tennessee with her husband Dave, a retired maintenance worker and electrician.

They have four children, Terrance, an IT Tech Specialist, DJ, a Police Sergeant, Kristie, a Primary Patent Engineer, and Kenneth a Truck Driver. They are the grandparents of 8 grandchildren and spiritual guardians to Julius and Florence Oyier and their 2 sons.

Georgia has begun her second book, sharing her blessings and challenges of a renewed faith and strength, as she journey compassionately beside her husband Dave, who was diagnosed with early stage Alzheimer's disease, July, 2018; with the prayerful support of their children.

CPSIA information can be obtained
at www.ICGtesting.com
Printed in the USA
LVHW091659291219
641984LV00002B/428/P

9 781644 589519